VOID

OUCH!

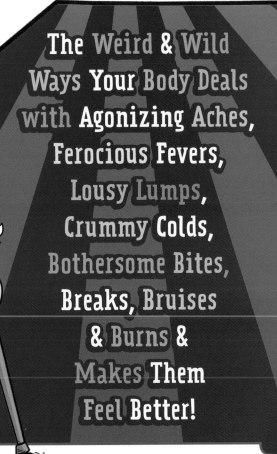

The Weird & Wild
Ways Your Body Deals
with Agonizing Aches,
Ferocious Fevers,
Lousy Lumps,
Crummy Colds,
Bothersome Bites,
Breaks, Bruises
& Burns &
Makes Them
Feel Better!

Joe Rhatigan

ILLUSTRATIONS BY ANTHONY OWSLEY

imagine!
Publishing

An Imagine Book
Published by Charlesbridge
85 Main Street, Watertown, MA 02472
(617) 926-0329
www.charlesbridge.com

Library of Congress Cataloging-in-Publication Data

Rhatigan, Joe.
  Ouch! : the weird & wild ways your body deals with agonizing aches, ferocious fevers, lousy lumps,
crummy colds, bothersome bites, breaks, bruises & burns & makes them feel better / Joe Rhatigan ;
original Illustrations by Anthony Owsley.
      pages cm
ISBN 978-1-62354-053-1
1. Pain—Popular works. 2. Psychology, Pathological. I. Title.
RB127.R52 2013
616'.0472—dc23

                        2012048462

2 4 6 8 10 9 7 5 3 1

For information about custom editions, special sales, premium and corporate purchases, please contact Charlesbridge
Publishing at specialsales@charlesbridge.com.

This book is dedicated to the doctors and nurses who helped fix my broken tibia, broken ankle, fractured skull, broken nose, broken clavicle, broken ankle (again), and assorted rashes, lumps, sprains, and illnesses. I'd be in a lot worse shape without you.

The contents of this book have been reviewed by Richard Hudspeth, MD, Faculty, Mountain Area Health Education Center (MAHEC), Family Medicine Residency Program, Hendersonville, NC

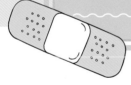

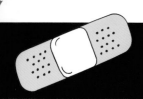

CONTENTS

INTRODUCTION

As you are reading these words, your body is performing thousands of functions. It's breathing, moving your eyes back and forth, understanding what this paragraph is describing, digesting lunch, fidgeting in the chair you're sitting in, worrying about tomorrow's math test, replacing dead cells, fighting the germs from the kid who sneezed on you ... I think you get the idea. Your body coordinates thousands of instructions so you can jump

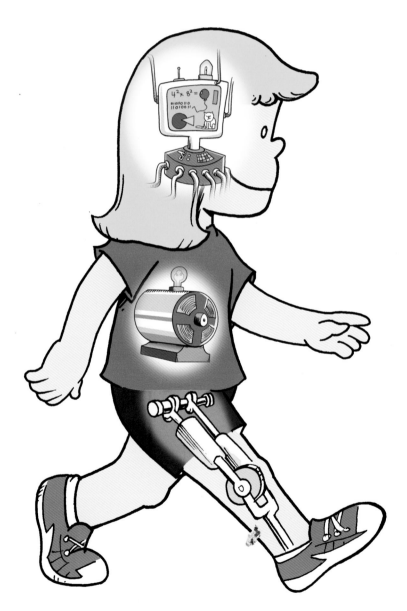

a jump rope or catch a football. It has systems in place to let you know when you're hungry, tired, in danger, and hurt. Like a machine that never shuts off, your body is constantly working to help you do all the things you need to do. And when everything is going smoothly, you hardly notice any of this at all! (Don't worry, your body doesn't mind.)

However, your body doesn't always have it easy. There are germs and other tiny invaders that can get to your healthy cells and destroy them. Accidents cause bumps, bruises, and breaks that slow down or stop part of the machine from functioning. But luckily, when these things happen, your body makes sure you take notice. How? By giving you pain, an ache, a bruise, an itch, or other irritation. Your body gets your attention quickly. Ouch!

Now, your body can take care of much of what comes its way. It employs microscopic warriors to destroy germs. It has armor to keep accidents from causing too much damage. From your blood to your eyelashes, your brain to your skin, your body is ready for just about anything. And when the body isn't up to the challenge, you, your parents, and your doctor help it do its job.

Ouch! is all about the times when you can't

ignore what's going on in your body—when something hurts. This book describes different ways you get injured and sick, and some of the things your body does and you, and your parents and doctors do to get all your body's systems back up and running. You'll explore the armor that keeps the bad stuff out, the warriors that attack the stuff that gets in, and the maintenance crew that cleans up the mess and heals you.

It's great to know about what's going on with your body and how to help it heal. For one thing, this knowledge helps you worry less when something goes wrong. Also, working with your body to help it get better means you'll heal or get cured more quickly . . . so the hurt will go away and you can go back to enjoying—and ignoring—your body as soon as possible.

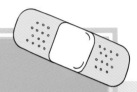

DISCLAIMER

This book is not a doctor. Do not use this book to try and figure out what's wrong with you. That's what your parents and doctors are for. Once you've been diagnosed, you can read up on what you have, what's going on with your body, and how you're going to get better. Always tell an adult when something is going wrong with your body, and don't take any medicines unless prescribed by a doctor or given to you by an adult you trust. This book doesn't give a lot of information on medications or alternative therapies. Your parents and doctors will decide what's best for your body, and when you're a little older, you'll make those decisions for yourself. One thing I will say, however, is that it's amazing what eating well, exercising regularly, and getting plenty of rest can do for you. You'll have more energy throughout the day, get sick less often, and heal faster. You'll spend less time in the doctor's office and more time doing the things you love.

Stay healthy!

BODY BASICS

It's a beautiful day and you decide to take your bike out for a ride. However, no matter how hard you push, the pedals won't budge. Is there a problem with the chain and cranks? The pedals and gears? Now, the more you know about bikes, the more likely it is that you'll be able to figure it out and fix the problem yourself. Well, the same thing goes with your body. Knowing how the body works and what it does when you're sick or hurt can help you make decisions about what to do when you skin your knee, catch a cold, or hurt your wrist. Knowing about your body also helps you decide when you need to get a parent involved and when you have to go to the doctor or hospital. Check out the body basics in this section and refer to them when reading about all the different ways your body hurts.

The Stuff That Makes Up Your Body

Like any machine, your body is made up of lots of small pieces, which come together to make bigger pieces, which, in turn, form even bigger pieces. These pieces all function together so that the machine of your body works just the way it's supposed to.

The Building Blocks

Cells are the smallest units of life and all living things are composed of one or more cells. Everything in your body is made up of cells, and your body has trillions of them. There's not just one kind of cell. In fact, there are more than 200 different kinds of cells in your body and each has a job to do, from building bone, muscles, and organs to fighting off germs, sending messages to and from your brain, and more. Cells divide and multiply in order to replace dead cells and so you can grow.

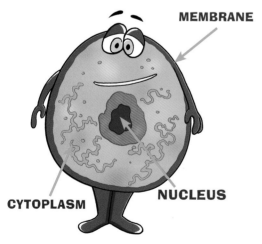

MEMBRANE

CYTOPLASM

NUCLEUS

Cells are composed of a thin skin-like covering called a membrane that protects a nucleus, the control center of the cell, and cytoplasm, a jellylike material that fills the cell.

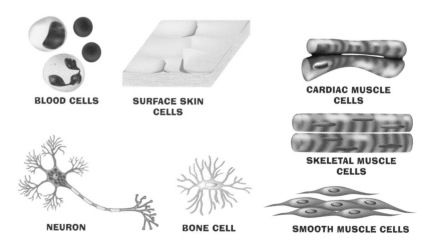

BLOOD CELLS

SURFACE SKIN CELLS

CARDIAC MUSCLE CELLS

SKELETAL MUSCLE CELLS

NEURON

BONE CELL

SMOOTH MUSCLE CELLS

Tissue

Tissue is a group of cells that perform a specific task. Types of tissue in your body include muscle tissue, nervous tissue, and connective tissue.

Organs

An organ consists of two or more types of tissue that work together to perform a task. Some of the organs in your body are your heart, liver, stomach, and skin.

System

A system is a group of organs that work together to perform a task. Your body's systems include:

CIRCULATORY
Parts: heart, lungs, blood, blood vessels
Job: to pump and move blood where it needs to go, bringing food and oxygen to each cell, carrying away waste, and transporting disease-fighting cells where they are needed

DIGESTIVE
Parts: stomach, liver, gallbladder, pancreas, esophagus, salivary glands, intestines, and more
Job: to process food and get rid of waste

ENDOCRINE
Parts: glands
Job: to help the body work properly through the use of hormones, which send information and instructions throughout the body

IMMUNE AND LYMPHATIC
Parts: lymph nodes, blood vessels, blood
Job: to drain excess fluid from all parts of your body and help fight infections

INTEGUMENTARY
Parts: skin, hair, fat, nails
Job: to protect the body

MUSCULAR
Parts: skeletal muscles (not including the internal muscles such as the heart)
Job: to produce movement and maintain posture

NERVOUS
Parts: brain, spinal cord, nerves
Job: to collect, send, and understand information from your environment/surroundings

REPRODUCTIVE
Parts: male and female sex organs
Job: to make babies

RESPIRATORY
Parts: lungs, diaphragm, larynx, and more
Job: to make it possible for you to breathe

SKELETAL
Parts: bones, cartilage, ligaments, tendons
Job: to support and protect the body

URINARY AND EXCRETORY
Parts: kidneys, bladder, and more
Job: to get rid of waste (urine) and keep your fluids balanced

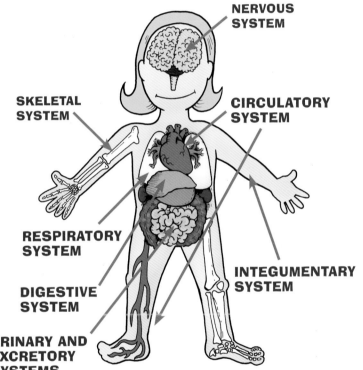

NERVOUS SYSTEM

SKELETAL SYSTEM

CIRCULATORY SYSTEM

RESPIRATORY SYSTEM

DIGESTIVE SYSTEM

INTEGUMENTARY SYSTEM

URINARY AND EXCRETORY SYSTEMS

Why Does It Hurt?

You roll out of bed and stub your toe. Ouch! You eat a spoonful of oatmeal that's way too hot and burn your tongue. Double ouch!! You trip running for the school bus and skin your knee. Triple ouch!!! Yes, you're having a tough morning, but if it weren't for pain, your day could be a lot worse.

Pain is a message from your body telling you to stop doing what you're doing and take care of yourself, to be careful next time, or to move your body away from danger. If banging your toe didn't hurt, you could be walking around with a broken bone and not even know it. If you kept eating that oatmeal without waiting for it to cool, you could burn your mouth and tongue, making it difficult to talk and eat. If you didn't wash your knee and put a bandage on it, you'd risk infection. And although you feel pain in different parts of your body, you can thank your brain and nervous system for those important pain messages.

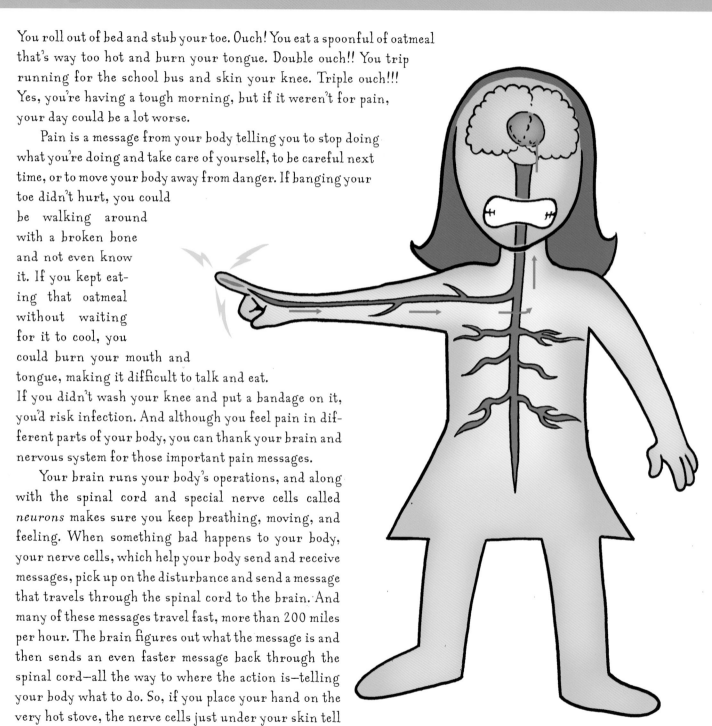

Your brain runs your body's operations, and along with the spinal cord and special nerve cells called *neurons* makes sure you keep breathing, moving, and feeling. When something bad happens to your body, your nerve cells, which help your body send and receive messages, pick up on the disturbance and send a message that travels through the spinal cord to the brain. And many of these messages travel fast, more than 200 miles per hour. The brain figures out what the message is and then sends an even faster message back through the spinal cord—all the way to where the action is—telling your body what to do. So, if you place your hand on the very hot stove, the nerve cells just under your skin tell

This illustration shows what the octopus-like neurons look like under a microscope.

your brain, and your brain tells your muscles to move that hand . . . quickly!

Your brain, spinal cord, and nerve cells are all part of what scientists call your *nervous system*, one of the groups of organs in your body that work together to perform tasks. This system controls all your movements, lets you experience pain and temperature, and makes sure everything in your body is working smoothly. Sure, without it you wouldn't feel any pain; however, you'd also be walking around wondering why your foot no longer moves correctly; why your mouth, tongue, and lips are puffy; and why your knee is swollen and turning black-and-blue.

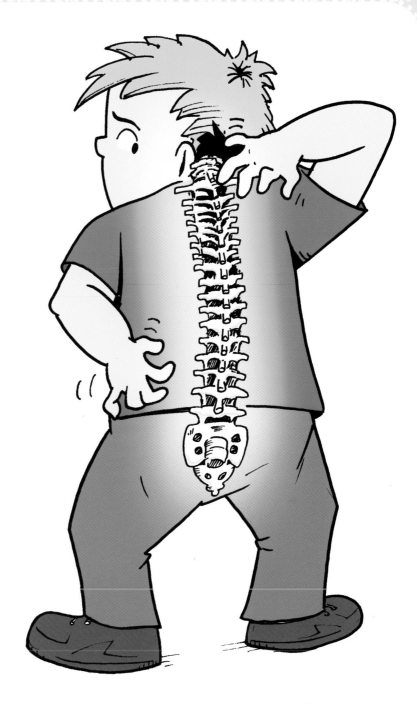

If your brain is the command center, your spinal cord is the information highway—a thick "wire" that delivers messages between your brain and the rest of your body. This highway has thirty-one smaller spinal nerves that branch off your spinal cord and are connected to even smaller "wires" that reach all the parts of your body. Your spinal cord is attached to the base of your brain and runs down your back.

The Ouch! Pain Scale

One of the ways doctors figure out what's wrong with their patients is to ask about their pain. Sometimes they'll use a pain scale such as the Wong-Baker FACES Pain Rating Scale to help. Instead of trying to describe how much it hurts, all you have to do is point to the face that best represents how much you're hurting. We've created our own pain scale so you can see how much all the hurts in this book actually hurt without getting hurt yourself!

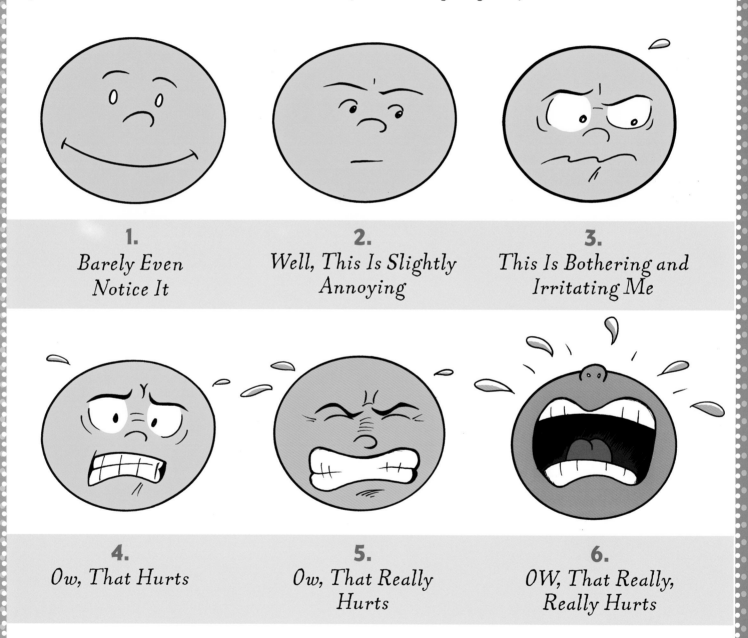

1.
Barely Even Notice It

2.
Well, This Is Slightly Annoying

3.
This Is Bothering and Irritating Me

4.
Ow, That Hurts

5.
Ow, That Really Hurts

6.
OW, That Really, Really Hurts

The First Line of Defense

It may not feel like it, but you're wearing full-body armor. It's covering just about every part of your body, protecting your insides from bacteria, viruses, dirt, germs, and more. (See page 19 for more on germs!) This armor isn't made of steel, but of skin. In fact, it *is* your skin, your body's biggest organ (weighing up to 16 percent of your total body weight), which acts as the first line of defense against all the bad stuff that's trying to get in and mess up your smooth-running machine. This organ is part of the integumentary system as well as part of a complicated system of cells, tissue, and organs called the immune system, which protects the body. You'll be reading more about this system throughout this book.

Your skin protects you from chocolate syrup.

Compared to a knight's armor, your skin may seem a tad flimsy and not up to the job, but these layers of tissue guard your muscles, bones, and internal organs; keep nutrients inside where *they* belong and germs and bacteria out where they belong; help you sense the outside world; keep you at just the right temperature; and more. Skin is flexible, letting you move, jump, stretch, and grow.

Your skin has three layers, each of which does a different job and protects you in unique ways.

Subcutaneous Fat

This is the bottom layer of your skin. It's made up mostly of fat, which provides insulation against cold or heat as well as cushioning for when you fall or get bumped. This layer attaches to bones and muscles.

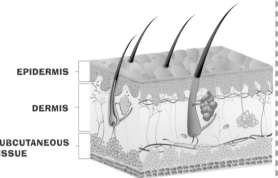

EPIDERMIS

DERMIS

SUBCUTANEOUS TISSUE

The Dermis

This is the middle layer of your skin. It's tough and stretchy and home to nerve endings, blood vessels, oil and sweat glands, and more. The blood vessels bring your skin cells the oxygen and nutrients they need to stay healthy and also take away waste. Oil glands produce a chemical called *sebum*, which rises to the epidermis and keeps the skin waterproof, lubricated, and protected. Sebum also provides protection against germs. The sweat glands produce sweat, which, along with blood flow rate, helps you regulate your temperature.

The Epidermis

This is the top layer of your skin. It is made up of dead cells that were once part of the lower skin layers. Your epidermis helps protect you from sun damage and keeps water and germs out. These dead cells continually fall from your skin, only to be replaced by new cells from below.

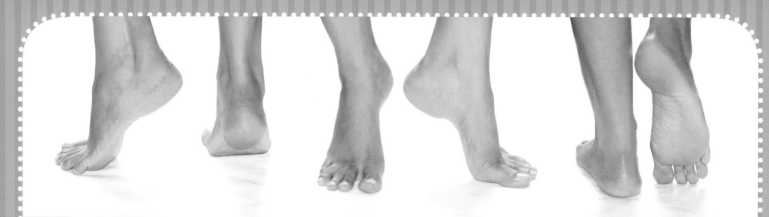

Skin isn't the same thickness everywhere. It is thinnest under the eyes (.5 mm thick) and around the eyelids and thickest on your palms and soles of your feet (up to 4 mm thick).

 (.5 mm thick) =========   (up to 4 mm thick) _____

Where There's No Skin

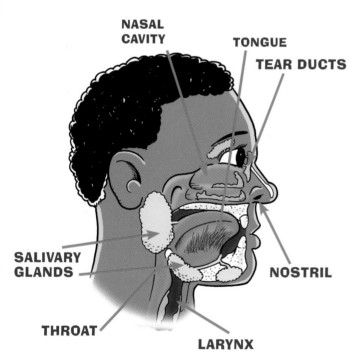

NASAL CAVITY

TONGUE

TEAR DUCTS

SALIVARY GLANDS

NOSTRIL

THROAT

LARYNX

Your nose, mouth, and eyes provide openings for germs to get in. Thankfully, each area has a form of protection to keep germs from attacking.

• A thick, sticky substance called *mucus* (otherwise known as *snot*) destroys some of the germ cells and also keeps them from going farther into your body. Mucus is found in your mouth, throat, nose, lungs, and bowels.

• The saliva in your mouth, otherwise known as *spit*, and tears in your eyes contain special chemicals that break down the cell walls of many bacteria and viruses.

• Mucus and saliva trap the germs in your nose and throat, and when swallowed, acids in the stomach kill the germs.

The major passages of the upper respiratory tract include the nose, nasal cavity, mouth, throat (pharynx), and voice box (larynx). The respiratory system is lined with a mucous membrane that secretes mucus. Hairlike structures called cilia line the mucous membrane and move the particles trapped in the mucus out of the nose.

A gooey germ-fighting machine!

The Warriors

Your skin protects all your insides—muscles, bones, ligaments, arteries, organs, and blood. And it keeps out much of the stuff that's supposed to stay out. But there are times when the skin just isn't up to the job. Germs, dirt, grime, and more get past the first line of defense and inside where they don't belong. That's when the warriors beneath your skin go to work. These warriors are all part of your immune system, and many of them live in your blood.

Blood is part of your body's circulatory system. Your heart pumps your blood and your network of blood vessels carry it throughout your body. There are special cells in your blood that help your body fight diseases called *white blood cells*. These cells are created in your *bone marrow*, the living tissue found inside many of your bones. Your bone marrow also makes red blood cells and platelets.

What Your Blood Is Made Of

PLASMA
More than half of your blood (around 55 percent) is made up of this pale yellow liquid, a mixture of mostly water, along with salt, nutrients, and more.

PLATELETS
These are tiny round cells that stop the bleeding when you have a cut.

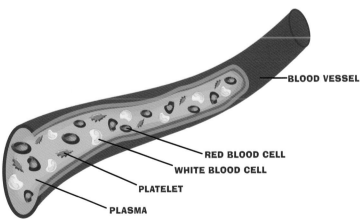

BLOOD VESSEL

RED BLOOD CELL

WHITE BLOOD CELL

PLATELET

PLASMA

RED BLOOD CELLS
These look like dodgeballs with the air taken out of them. Red blood cells are red because of a chemical called *hemoglobin*, which carries oxygen from your lungs to your body's cells and then carries wastes such as carbon dioxide from the cells back to the lungs.

WHITE BLOOD CELLS

These cells are bigger than red blood cells, and it's their job to fight the invading germs that get in from the outside. They are produced by stem cells in your bone marrow and are found in your blood and your lymphatic system. There are different types of white blood cells, each of which has an important function.

Granulocytes

These are the body's main defense against bacteria. They get rid of germs by ingesting them in a process called *phagocytosis*. Most of the granulocytes are *neutrophils*, which are the first white blood cells to arrive at a site of an injury. Each neutrophil can phagocytize from five to twenty bacteria before dying. There are more neutrophils in your body than any other type of white blood cell. Other granulocytes are responsible for killing parasites and protozoa. Another granulocyte is responsible for releasing histamine, which causes blood vessels to leak, attracting white blood cells to the scene. Histamine is what causes allergic reactions (see page 66).

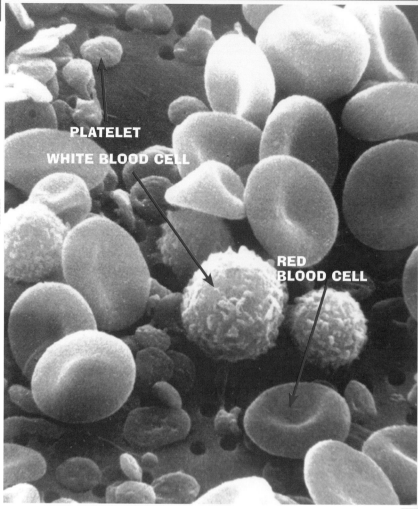

PLATELET

WHITE BLOOD CELL

RED BLOOD CELL

This is what your blood looks like under an electron microscope.

Monocytes

These are the largest of the white blood cells. Once released by the bone marrow, they move to the blood and then into tissue, where they turn into *macrophages*. These serve as a general cleanup service for different organs. For example, macrophages will remove smoke particles from your lungs. They also surround invading germs that have escaped the neutrophils, swallow them up (up to 100 each), and clean up the neutrophils that died fighting germs. The pus that forms in infected cuts is dead neutrophils.

Lymphocytes

These guys also fight bacterial and viral infections, but instead of swallowing them, they recognize and remember them. When your body is infected with a particular germ, only the lymphocytes that recognize it will attack by multiplying quickly, creating an army to fight off the germ. The next time this germ comes around, a few lymphocytes remember it and attack it before it can multiply, making you *immune* to the disease, which means you can't get infected by that same virus again.

A single drop of blood has around 9,000 white blood cells, 250,000 platelets, and 5 million red blood cells.

The Bad Guys

So, who are these bad guys that are just dying to get in our bodies and make us miserable? They're called germs, pathogens, or infectious agents and they're the microscopic organisms that can cause diseases. There are trillions and trillions of germs in the air, water, and soil; on plants and animals; in your hair; on your fingers; in your stomach and mouth. Germs can be broken down into four categories—viruses, bacteria, fungi, and protozoa. Certain members of each of these categories can harm you, though not all of them are bad for you or cause any problems at all. When germs invade your body and multiply, it's called getting an *infection*.

Bacteria

These are one-celled organisms that are much smaller than one of your own cells. Bacteria can exist on their own and like to live and eat inside our bodies. Most bacteria are harmless or even good for you, but some can cause diseases such as strep throat, ear infections, and pneumonia. If you have a bacterial infection, it will usually be in one place in or on your body, and you may be prescribed a certain type of medicine called an *antibiotic*. An antibiotic's job is to kill bacteria and help you feel better more quickly.

Viruses

A virus isn't technically alive, and therefore can't reproduce on its own. In order to make copies of itself, a virus particle, otherwise known as a *virion*, takes over a cell, which then reproduces with the virus inside it. This is how a virus spreads through your body. Chicken pox, measles, the flu, and the common cold are all viruses. Antibiotics cannot cure viruses; however, there are antiviral medicines that combat them. Viruses tend to affect many different parts of the body at once.

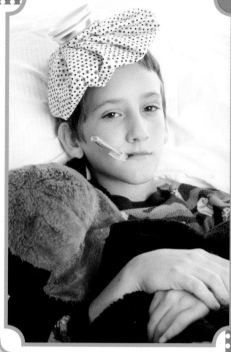

Protozoa

Protozoa are one-celled organisms that can live wherever there is some moisture (water, damp soil, etc.). These cause infections in our intestines, leading to stomachaches, diarrhea, and vomiting.

Don't drink the water! Even if stream, lake, or river water looks clean and pure, it can still be contaminated with bacteria, viruses, and protozoa. Always bring your own water with you when camping or hiking.

Fungi

Fungi are multicelled plantlike creatures that live in warm, damp places, such as between your toes. Athlete's foot is a common fungal attack.

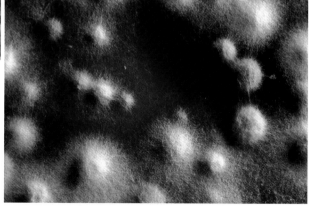

This is what athlete's foot fungus looks like under a microscope.

Staphylococcus aureus   *Streptococcus pyogenes*

Streptococcus pneumoniae

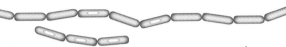

Bacillus cereus

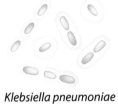

Klebsiella pneumoniae

Vibrio cholerae

E. coli ; Salmonella

Bordetella pertussis   *Corynebacterium diphtheriae*   *Helicobacter pylori*

Clostridium botulinum   *Clostridium tetani*   *Neisseria gonorrhoeae*   *Treponema pallidum*

Different types of bacteria.

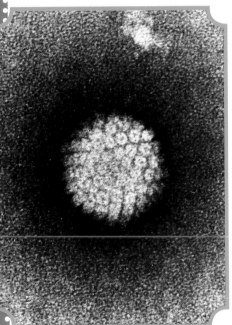

This virus, photographed using an electron microscope, causes warts.

THE INJURIES, INFECTIONS, AND OTHER THINGS THAT CAN GO WRONG

Most of the time, your body is very good at keeping things running smoothly; however, there are also a variety of ways to hurt yourself or get sick. For each of the injuries, infections, and ouches listed in this section, I will describe:

— The *symptoms*, or what the injury or sickness looks and feels like
— Your *first response*, or what you should do as soon as you're hurt or sick
— What your doctor will say or do to help your body recover
— What your body is doing to heal itself and help you feel better
— What you can do to prevent this injury or sickness from happening in the first place or to keep the injury or illness from getting worse.

Note: *The Ouch! Pain Scale* for each injury in this section provides only a *general idea* of what the pain associated with the ouch may be. Your own experience may be more or less painful.

FIRST, DO NO HARM

Medical students around the world often recite an oath when they graduate in which they promise to treat the sick as best as they can, keep patients' information private, teach the profession to others, and also, to first do no harm. This is called the Hippocratic Oath, named after the father of Western medicine, the fifth-century BCE Greek physician, Hippocrates. The next time you're at the doctor's office, see if you can find the oath somewhere on the wall.

Ugh! There's Something Stuck in My Skin!

Imagine you're walking barefoot across a wooden deck or moving your hand across an unfinished wood surface, when all of a sudden, a thin piece of wood gets stuck in the upper layer of your skin. That thin piece of wood is called a *splinter*. Some splinters hurt; other times you may not even realize you have one.

First Response

A parent can help you remove a splinter safely. If a part of the splinter is sticking out of the skin, you can use a pair of tweezers to get it out. Or, place a piece of cellophane tape over the splinter and then pull the tape off. If you're lucky, the tape will take the splinter out with it.

If the splinter is in too deeply to grab with tweezers, have a parent clean a needle with alcohol and then use it to create a small hole in the skin directly over the end of the splinter that's closest to the surface of your skin. Then your parent should use the needle to lift the splinter until he or she can grab it with tweezers and take it out.

Once the splinter is gone, clean the area with soap and water and cover it with a bandage.

What Your Doctor Does

You won't need to see a doctor unless the splinter is deep in the skin, if it's bleeding badly, or it's pretty big. The doctor may use a medicine called *anesthesia* to numb the area before removing the splinter.

What Your Body Does

If you decide to leave a wood splinter alone because it's not hurting and it's near the surface of the skin, your body may get rid of it for you. The splinter can work its way out as new skin grows and pushes out the old, dead skin holding the splinter out.

What You Can Do to Prevent Splinters

The best way to avoid splinters is to wear shoes when traveling over wooden surfaces such as decks and boardwalks and to keep from rubbing your hand over wooden railings and playground structures.

From *Barely Even Notice It* to *Ow, That Really Hurts* on the Ouch! Pain Scale

Eeew! A Gooey, Ooey Blister!

A blister is a liquid-filled sack that forms on the top layer of your skin. Some blisters are caused by friction. For example, if you go on a hike while wearing a pair of shoes that are a little too big for you, the friction of the shoe rubbing against the back of your foot over and over may cause a blister to form there. Each step can become painful, especially if the blister pops and the raw lower layers of skin beneath are exposed. (Blisters can also be caused by burns, which will be discussed further on page 34.)

First Response

If your blister is caused by friction, the best thing to do is simply leave it alone. It will heal all by itself. You shouldn't even put a bandage on it unless it's the only way to reduce the friction between the skin and whatever is rubbing against it. So, if you're only halfway through your hike, put a bandage over the blister to keep it from getting worse. If the blister is on the bottom of your foot, use a doughnut-shaped pad that goes around the blister, leaving the actual blistered area open.

Since blisters can become infected pretty easily, always wash your hands before touching one. If the blister breaks on its own, don't remove the flap of skin. You can apply an antibiotic ointment and a bandage so the area doesn't get infected.

What Your Doctor Does

If your blister is caused by friction, you won't need to see a doctor.

What Your Body Does

Your body forms a blister in order to protect and cushion the skin tissue underneath, giving it a chance to heal. The clear liquid inside is called *serum*. Serum keeps the area infection free until new outer skin can form. Serum isn't water, but is made up of components of your blood, minus the red blood cells, which give your blood the red color.

What You Can Do to Prevent Blisters

To avoid getting friction blisters on your feet, wear shoes that fit, along with clean socks. Blisters tend to form in moist conditions so it's important to either find socks that wick away moisture or to change your socks when your feet get sweaty or soaked. Your hands are another common place for blisters. Wear gloves when doing yard work or whenever you're using tools or sports equipment such as hockey sticks or baseball bats.

Well, This Is Slightly Annoying on the Ouch! Pain Scale

NEXT TIME, LET'S TRY USING SOME GLOVES AND SHOES!

Bummer! I'm Black-and-Blue!

It's easy to tell when you have a bruise because your skin turns a weird shade of black-and-blue, which is why a bruise is sometimes called a . . . black-and-blue. From bumping your leg on a chair to getting hit in the arm by a baseball, there are lots of ways to get bruises. If you get banged or bumped, there's always a chance you'll get one. In fact, depending on how active (or clumsy) you are, at any given moment, you may have more than one on your body. The good news is that nearly all of the time, bruises are nothing to get too worried about. Your body takes care of them with no help from doctors or even from you!

Your skin usually protects your insides. Sometimes, however, the bang or bump is hard enough to injure the muscles and tissue under the skin without breaking it. Small veins and capillaries (see page 29) break, leaking out red blood cells, which collect closer to it, causing the black-and-blue coloring. The injured area will be sensitive to the touch. The harder the bang, the more the area will hurt and the longer it will take for the bruise to go away. Within a week or two, the area should look as good as new.

The lighter your skin, the more prominent your bruise.

I call a bruise a contusion.

First Response

If it's a mild bruise, you can pretty much ignore it. If you act fast, you can help reduce any swelling and the amount of bruising by applying a cold compress to the area for ten to fifteen minutes. This slows down the blood flowing into the area. Elevating the area will also help.

What Your Doctor Does

Doctors are not needed for mild bruises. Serious bruises are usually a sign that something else is going on, such as a fracture, in which case you'll definitely be visiting a doctor. Other reasons to seek a doctor include a bruise that doesn't go away, a bruise getting more painful as time goes by, and an especially large bruise, or if you're getting bruised a lot but you're not bumping or banging into anything.

What Your Body Does

Once the red blood cells have escaped the capillaries and have pooled under the skin, they eventually die and turn darker in color, which is why your bruise changes colors as well. Then, white blood cells get into the act, disposing of the dead cells.

What You Can Do to Prevent Bruises

There isn't much you can do to avoid everyday bangs and bumps; however, make sure you're wearing the proper protective gear when playing sports and riding your bike or skateboard.

From *Barely Even Notice It* to *OW, That Really, Really Hurts* on the Ouch! Pain Scale

BRUISE CHART

Track your bruises using this handy chart!

First day	Your bruise will look red and may swell as red blood cells collect in the injured area.
Second day through fifth day	Any swelling will go down and the bruise will look blue, black, and/or deep purple. (The color changes as the red blood cells begin to decay, turning your injury a darker color.)
After five days or so	Your bruise may turn green or yellow as your white blood cells clean up the mess and dispose of the decaying red blood cells.
After ten days	Your bruise will be light brown and then get lighter and lighter until it disappears, usually after about two weeks.

BLACK EYE

Like other bruises on your body, a black eye usually looks worse than it is. If your face gets banged or bumped, red blood cells will collect under the skin and around the eye. Most black eyes aren't serious and will heal in about a week.

ABOUT CAPILLARIES

Inside your body is a vast system of blood vessels, which are in charge of sending blood to and from your heart and other body parts. This is called your circulatory system. Arteries, which look red, carry blood away from the heart. Veins, which usually look blue, return the blood to the heart. These arteries and veins are like a confusing map with hundreds of highways and roads passing under, over, and around one another. Capillaries, meanwhile, are the tiny roads that connect the arteries and veins. Capillaries are quite thin (only one cell thick) and fragile, which is why they often break when you get bumped. By the way, if you took out all of your blood vessels and laid them end to end in a straight line (not something I advise doing), the line would be at least 60,000 miles long, enough to wrap around Earth more than two times!

Help! I'm Bleeding!

Your skin performs well when bumped and pinched; however, a sharp knife, broken glass, a pair of scissors, or even the edge of a piece of paper can easily pierce your armor. The first sign that your skin has failed is blood, which will come flowing out of the injured area. You will also feel pain as your nerve endings and brain send messages informing you of what to do.

If the cut isn't too deep or large, the bleeding will stop fairly quickly. Larger cuts take longer to stop bleeding and you may need stitches to close the wound.

First Response

If there seems to be a lot of blood, seek medical attention immediately. If the cut is minor, first, stop the bleeding by pressing a clean cloth against the wound for a minute or two. Then, clean it with soap and warm water—making sure to remove any dirt or grime that is in the damaged area of skin. (This can be difficult with abrasions—see page 31.) Once clean, an adult can apply an antibacterial ointment to the wound to keep germs from infecting the area, and then, apply a bandage.

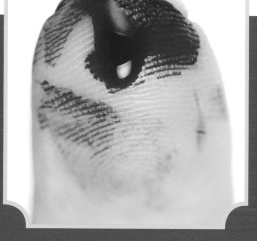

THREE TYPES OF SKIN INJURIES

CUT—a slice in the skin, usually the result of penetration by a sharp object

SCRATCH—usually less serious than a cut, a scratch is the result of a sharp object scraping against the skin and just barely penetrating the first few layers

ABRASION—a raw area of the skin that occurs when multiple layers of the skin are rubbed away, often the result of a fall. A skinned knee is a common (and painful!) type of abrasion.

An abrasion.

What Your Doctor Does

You will only need to go to a doctor if the bleeding doesn't stop after several minutes or if the wound becomes severely infected. Deeper wounds may require extra help in the form of stitches, staples, or a special glue. If you go to the doctor for a skin injury, here's what might happen: First, your doctor will numb the injured area with an anesthetic. (This usually requires a shot.) Then, she will sew the edges of the cut together with a special type of needle and thread, or *suture*. This is called *suturing* the wound. Depending on the type of stitches, they will either dissolve on their own after a few weeks or you'll have to return to the doctor to have them removed once the wound has healed. Your doctor may use a glue called *dermal adhesive* instead of stitches. This holds the sides of the injury together and dissolves once the wound is healed.

What Your Body Does

As sharp objects pierce the skin, blood vessels are cut and you bleed. This is a signal for your blood to spring into action. The platelets in your blood stick to the edge of the wound and one another while they pile up in a clump to stop the bleeding. The blood at the surface turns into a sort of jelly and soon dries into a scab. This is called *coagulation*. Meanwhile, the white blood cells are fighting off any germs that may have entered through the cut. Damaged blood vessels begin repairing themselves, and skin cells grow under the scab. In a week or two (depending on how deep the cut was) all that will be left is a scar, which is the new skin that bridged the two sides of the cut together. Some scars fade away after a while. Others will stick around forever.

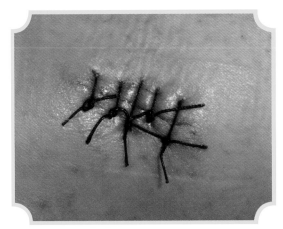

Stitches.

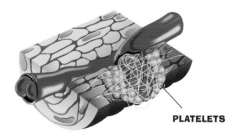

INJURED BLOOD VESSEL

COAGULATION

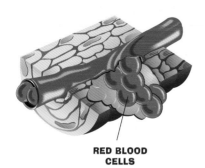

RED BLOOD
CELLS

PLATELETS

What You Can Do to Prevent Cuts

The best thing you can do is treat sharp objects with care and wear the proper gear when playing sports. When your skin is injured, acting quickly helps prevent excessive blood loss and decreases your risk of getting an infection.

From *Well, This Is Slightly Annoying* to *OW, That Really, Really Hurts* on the Ouch! Pain Scale

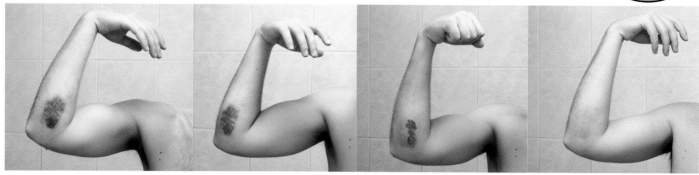

An abrasion healing over time.

DON'T PICK IT!

The hard, crusty layer that forms over your cut is called a *scab*. Some people find it hard to keep from picking at their scabs, but doing so makes the healing take longer. Pulling off the scab can open the wound again, and then your blood and skin cells have to start all over. This can also lead to permanent scarring.

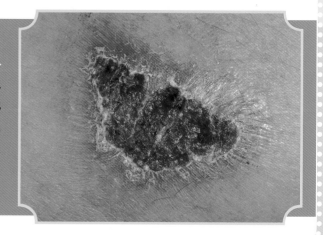

ICK! MY CUT'S INFECTED!

Most cuts and scratches are no big deal. However, sometimes there are too many germs for your white blood cells to handle and your wound gets infected. An infected cut looks red and swollen, feels warm to the touch, and often contains pus, which is a thick yellow or green liquid. Your body responds by raising the temperature around the wound, and sometimes your whole body will get warmer and you'll develop a fever. (See more on fevers on page 58.) Meanwhile, your white blood cells continue to fight the germs as well as eat away at the pus. Your doctor may prescribe an antibiotic to help your body. She may also need to reopen the wound to drain the pus. Antibiotics work quickly and can kill most of the bacteria in a few days. The one problem with antibiotics is that, over time, they lose their effectiveness in killing certain bacteria. That's because bacteria can change, or *mutate,* and become immune to the drug. Then, stronger antibiotics are needed.

I'VE BEEN BITTEN BY A KITTEN!

If an animal bites or scratches you and breaks your skin, not only will it hurt but the animal's germs can get into your body. If this happens, your doctor may prescribe an antibiotic to prevent infection and kill off the bacteria. If you've been bitten or scratched by a wild animal, your doctor might also be worried about a viral infection called *rabies.* If the wound needs help closing, your doctor will also give you stitches (see page 31).

THERE ARE NEARLY
FIVE MILLION
REPORTED DOG BITES IN
THE U.S. EVERY YEAR.

Ow! I Burned Myself!

There are lots of ways to get burned. Some of them include picking up a hot saucepan without an oven mitt, touching a hot curling iron, touching an exposed electrical wire, taking a too-hot shower, and spending too much time in the sun. When you get burned, one or more layers of your skin is destroyed. How serious your burn is depends on how hot the heat or flame is and how long your skin touched it. Your nervous system sends near-instant messages (Pain!) to the burned area so you will remove your skin from the source of the burn, but your skin can get damaged just as quickly.

While many burns will hurt right away, sunburns can be a bit different. They take a while to develop, so if you're out in the sun and your skin is getting burned, you might not notice until it's already too late! That's why it's important to put on sunblock and stay out of the sun during its peak hours, whether or not you feel yourself getting burned.

DEGREES OF BURNS

There are four major types of burns:

Type of Burn	Symptoms	Possible Causes	Healing Time
First Degree (only affects the epidermis)	Red, tender, and sore skin	Sunburn, scald, small open flame	Two to five days
Second Degree (affects the epidermis and dermis)	White, pink, and red skin; swelling; and oozing blisters	Bad sunburn, scald, open flame, chemicals	Anywhere from five days to one month
Third Degree (destroys the epidermis and dermis)	Charred appearance, skin leathery and dry	Long exposure to open flame, hot surfaces, hot liquids, electricity, chemicals	Could take months and you will have some scarring
Fourth Degree (injures tissue underneath the skin)	Black and charred	These often occur with electrical burns	Could take months

First Response

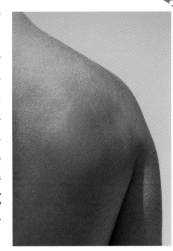

Mild burns (first-degree burns covering a small area) can be treated at home, but the more serious burns need to be taken care of by your doctor. The first thing to do with a mild burn is to run cool water over it for a few minutes. This stops the burning and helps numb the pain and reduce swelling. Do not use ice, which may restrict blood flow to the injured area. You can also cover the burn with a cold, wet towel. Do not use butter, oil, or sprays on the burn. After you have spent the proper amount of time cooling the burn, cover it with a loose bandage or clean cloth. Your parents can give you pain medication, which slows the swelling of the blood vessels (causing inflammation). For any serious burn or burn that covers a large area of your skin, seek medical attention as soon as possible.

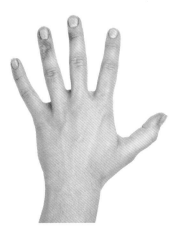

What Your Doctor Does

Severe burns (blistering over a large area and worse) need to be taken care of by a doctor. He will clean the wound of dead skin and dirt and perhaps apply an antibiotic cream and other medicines over the wound. If he thinks the burn won't heal on its own, you might need an operation called a *skin graft*, where a healthy piece of skin is taken from an unburned area and sewn over the burned area.

What Your Body Does

Whatever the damage, your body will quickly get to work repairing it. Sometimes, a blister will form over the injured area, protecting it from germs. Under that, your blood gets to work healing the burn much the same way it heals cuts and scrapes.

What You Can Do to Prevent Burns

One of the best ways to avoid burns is to make sure you and your family are aware of the potential ways any of you can get burned and take the proper precautions. Here are some examples of ways you can help protect your family (but this is by no means a complete list): Turn pot handles toward the back or center of the stove. Keep towels and napkins away from the stove to prevent fires. Turn off and unplug appliances when not in use. Ask a parent to help you check the wires around the house—especially if you have a pet that likes to chew things. And always protect your skin if spending time in the sun.

From *Ow, That Hurts* to *OW, That Really, Really Hurts* on the Ouch! Pain Scale

Uh-oh! I'm Bumpy and Lumpy All Over!

Lots of rashes may look and feel pretty much the same, but all sorts of different things can cause your skin to break out in itchy red bumps. Maybe you're allergic to something. Or perhaps your skin came into contact with something irritating such as a chemical or a soap. You could have a fever or a virus. And sometimes, you may never know for sure what caused your rash.

A Few Kinds of Rashes

ECZEMA

The symptoms of eczema are red, itchy, flaky, and swollen skin, usually showing up around your elbows or knees, although it can appear other places as well. Scientists don't know exactly why some people get this common rash. For those who suffer from eczema, it shows up and disappears at different times. Children who get eczema usually stop getting it by the time they're in their teens. Extreme cases of this rash require the help of parents and doctors to control it.

HIVES

Hives are swollen spots that are red or pale in color. If you've broken out in hives, it means your body is responding to something you're allergic to and is releasing a chemical called *histamine*. Many things including food, medicine, or a bug bite can trigger hives.

HEAT RASH

These small blister-like bumps can appear in areas where you've been sweating a lot.

IRRITANT DERMATITIS

Harsh soaps, detergents, chemicals, and overexposure to the sun can cause red, swollen rashes.

First Response

If you have a rash, the best thing to do is get to your doctor, so you can figure out what kind of rash you have. If your rash is itchy, your first instinct will probably be to scratch it. Don't do it! Scratching can spread the rash or lead to infection.

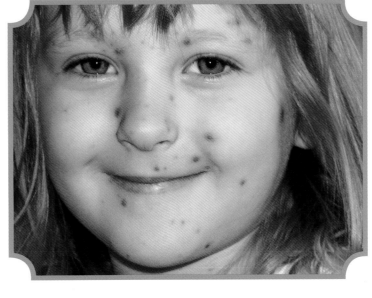

What Your Doctor Does

Depending on how serious your rash is, your doctor may send you to a special skin doctor called a *dermatologist*. The dermatologist will figure out what kind of rash you have and how to treat it. She may prescribe a moisturizer called an *emollient* if you have eczema. This will help your skin retain water. Your doctor may also prescribe a steroid cream. If you have hives, the doctor will spend some time trying to figure out what caused the allergic reaction, so you can avoid the allergen in the future. (See page 66 for more on allergies.)

What Your Body Does

A rash is usually a sign that something is invading your body. Immune system cells are quickly called into action to kill the invaders, and this can lead to inflammation of the skin. Once the invaders have been neutralized, your skin will return to normal.

What You Can Do to Prevent Rashes

For allergic rashes or irritant dermatitis, your best course of action is to avoid whatever caused your rash. For eczema, stay away from soaps that may dry out your skin. Use moisturizers or other medicines, even when you don't have a rash, and take cool showers, which won't dry out your skin.

I call rashes *dermatitis*.

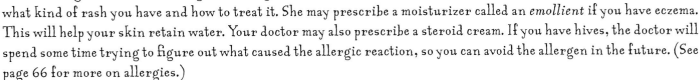

This Is Bothering and Irritating Me on the Ouch! Pain Scale

Argh! I've Been Poisoned by a Plant!

Who knew that one little plant could cause so much itching and misery!? One little touch from the plant known as poison ivy could lead to a rash that itches like crazy. Red, raised, and itchy bumps and blisters that ooze will form within twenty-four hours of contact with the oil the plant produces (*urushiol*), and it will take two weeks (sometimes longer) for the rash to go away.

First Response

Remove your outer garments as soon as you can because the oil can reside on your clothes and then make contact with your skin. Then, wash your hands and the infected area before poison ivy sets in. That means knowing what poison ivy looks like and washing off its poison before your body reacts to it. If you end up with a rash, use a cold compress to relieve the itching. Also, have a parent apply to the infected area one of the several over-the-counter medications that help relieve the symptoms.

What Your Doctor Does

You won't necessarily have to go to the doctor unless the rash shows up in sensitive areas or covers a large part of your body. Your doctor may prescribe an *antihistamine*, which will counteract the histamine your body has produced because of the allergy.

What Your Body Does

See the section on rashes on page 36.

What You Can Do to Prevent Poison Ivy

Know what poison ivy looks like. Its leaves are tear-shaped and grow in groups of three. The leaves are shiny and change color, so they can be green, red, or purple. Know where poison ivy might be and if you know you've touched some, don't touch anything else until you wash the area with soap and water. Also, wear closed shoes, socks, long pants, and long-sleeved shirts when hiking or camping where poison ivy is known to be present.

From *This Is Bothering and Irritating Me* to *Ow, That Really Hurts* on the Ouch! Pain Scale

Poison ivy is found in the U.S., east of the Rocky Mountains.

There are two other common plants that also produce urushiol. In the western part of the U.S., watch out for poison oak, which is a small tree or vine with leaves that also grow in groups of three. Poison sumac is found in the southeast U.S., and it is a tall shrub with thirteen to seventeen pointed leaves on each branch.

Poison ivy

Poison oak

Poison sumac

Imagine you're at the park with some friends tossing a Frisbee around when all of a sudden it feels like you just got poked in the arm with a needle. It hurts about as much as when you get a shot at the doctor's office, which means it isn't pleasant at all! You drop the Frisbee to look at what happened and there's a small something sticking out of your arm. It's a bee stinger and you've just been stung! Honeybees serve an important role in nature—they help pollinate plants and they make honey—but it sure is a pain getting stung by one of these guys.

At first, the area where you were stung will feel itchy and hot. It will get swollen, and a red bump with a white center will rise around the sting. It will hurt a lot at first, but after a few minutes, it will just feel achy. Meanwhile, under the skin, a venom sac from the bee's abdomen is pumping poison into your body. But don't worry. For most people, a bee sting is annoying and painful, but mostly harmless.

First Response

Have an adult help you remove the stinger as quickly as possible because it will keep pumping venom into your body for up to sixty seconds after a sting! The best way to do this is to scrape it out with a fingernail or something with a straight edge, such as a credit card. If you try to remove the stinger by pinching it, you'll just release more venom.

Next, wash the area with soap and warm water. Apply some ice, and that should be it. Some people, however, are allergic to bee stings, and they (or their parents) have to keep special medicine nearby at all

times. If someone is allergic to bee stings and is stung, they'll need to receive an injection of a special medicine right away so that their body's allergic reaction to the sting (see page 66) doesn't become too serious. If you've never been stung by a bee before (or if you've only been stung once before) make sure to tell an adult if you get a bee sting. You may not be aware that you're allergic, but if you are, it can be serious and adults will need to act quickly if you start having a reaction.

What Your Doctor Does

If the redness and swelling don't go away after a few days, your doctor may prescribe an antihistamine, which blocks the chemicals that are causing the irritation. If you're allergic to a bee sting, the medicine you need if you get stung is called *epinephrine*.

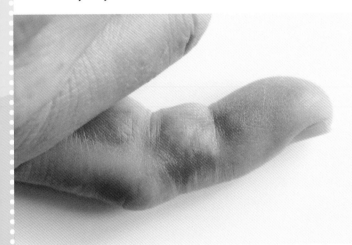

What Your Body Does

As soon as you have been stung, your body leaps into action. Nerve endings under your skin react to the stinger's piercing of your skin, sending an instant message to your brain, which then sends out a pain signal. That signal gets your attention and lets you know where you're hurt. At the same time, arteries carrying oxygen-rich blood expand to increase blood flow to the area of the attack, and the extra blood turns the area red while it hurls white blood cells at any germs that get in.

What You Can Do to Prevent Bee Stings

Honeybees don't want to sting you and will really only do so if they are swatted at or stepped on. In other words, if you leave a bee alone, it will leave you alone. You can also wear long pants and a long-sleeved shirt if you want. Avoiding bright-colored clothing can help keep the bees away. Also, avoid wearing scented lotions, perfumes, and soaps. Finally, don't kill and crush bees. The dead insect emits a smell that attracts more bees!

Ow, That Hurts on the Ouch! Pain Scale

WHAT HAPPENS IF YOU'RE ALLERGIC?

The symptoms if you're allergic to bee stings are more serious. They include tightness of the throat, difficulty breathing, stomachache, lightheadedness, hives, and more. If not treated quickly, you could have a seizure. Only around one in every 1,000 people is allergic to bee stings.

WHY DO BEES LEAVE THEIR STINGER BEHIND?

Honeybees have barbed stingers that get stuck in your skin as the bee pulls away. The bee ends up flying off without its stinger and its stomach, and it dies soon after.

DIFFERENCES BETWEEN BEES & WASPS

- Wasps are more aggressive and will go after you for little reason.
- Honeybees have round hairy bodies with flat rear legs. Wasps are smooth, shiny, and slender, and have a narrow waist connecting their middle and rear segments.
- Honeybees make their food (honey) from pollen and nectar from plants, while wasps make their food from other insects' blood as well as nectar.
- Honeybees build their nests out of wax, while wasps build theirs out of a paper-like pulp.
- Wasps (and some types of bees) can remove their stingers from your skin after stinging you.

Did you know a yellow jacket is a wasp and not a bee?

Oomph! I Broke a Bone!

Bones are pretty awesome things to have. For one thing, they keep you from being a formless, immobile blob of organs and skin. For another, they protect your insides from injury, help make blood, work with other body parts so you can move, and provide calcium, an important chemical for your body.

Bones can withstand a lot of force, so when you run, jump, play, and lift heavy things, they are more than up to the task. However, if a bone is put under intense or sudden pressure—more than it can handle—it may crack or break into two or more pieces. Falling from a bicycle, skateboard, or ladder can cause such pressure, especially if you land on a leg or an arm. Bumping into or getting hit by something hard can also break a bone.

How Will You Know a Bone Is Broken?

- It's going to hurt.
- You may have heard a "snap" during the fall or accident.
- The area where it hurts will swell up. You may also see a bump or the injured area will simply look different.
- Moving the injured area hurts. If it's your leg, you'll have difficulty putting pressure on it when you stand.
- In some cases, the bone may break through the skin. If this happens, there's no doubt about it: You have a serious or compound fracture.

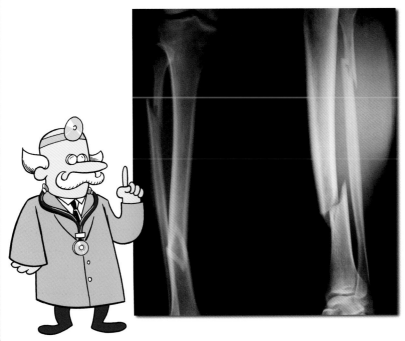

I call a broken bone a fracture.

• 43 •

THEY'RE ALIVE!

The bones you see in museums are dead, hard, and look easy to break. However, *your* bones are *alive* and growing. Breaking an old dead bone is like snapping a dead branch. Breaking one of your bones is like trying to snap a healthy living branch. It's much more difficult to do.

First Response

First, stop trying to move the hurt body part. Sometimes, people who are trying to be helpful suggest you do it. Don't listen to them. Then, have an adult place a cloth-wrapped ice pack or compress over the area. Seek immediate medical attention.

What Your Doctor Does

Your doctor will examine your injury and, based on what she finds, may take an X-ray to determine how serious the break is and whether it needs to be set. If the bone is broken into two pieces and the broken pieces aren't right up next to each other, the doctor may have to move the pieces until they are next to each other (aligned) so they can heal correctly. If your broken bone needs to be set, you will be given a medicine that puts you to sleep so you won't feel it when the bones are moved into a better location. Sometimes the doctor may insert pins or screws to keep the bones together while it heals.

Once the doctor has determined the bones are in the best position to heal, she will place the area in a splint or a cast. A splint is a piece of plastic or metal that can be molded to fit the injured area. You'll often see splints encasing broken fingers. These can be removed and replaced. A cast, on the other hand, isn't going anywhere until that bone is healed. These days, most casts are made of moldable plastic or fiberglass. The injured area is first wrapped in a few layers of soft cotton. Then, the cast material is soaked in water until it can be wrapped around the cotton. After a few hours, the material hardens, giving your injury the extra armor it needs to heal.

For a few days after the accident, you may be asked to elevate your broken bone to keep the swelling down. If your arm is broken, you may be given a sling, which is a piece of cloth attached to a strap that acts as a sleeve to keep the arm from moving around too much. If you broke a leg, you may be given a pair of crutches to use so you don't put any pressure on the injury.

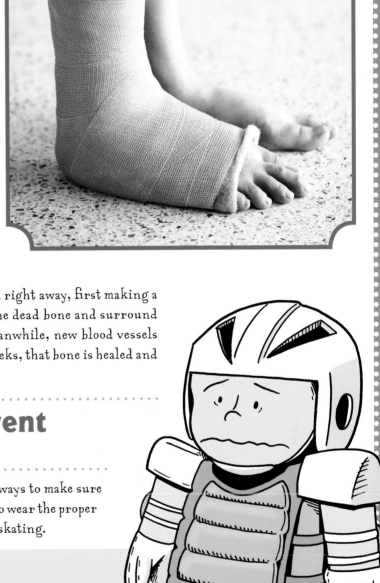

Depending on how severe the fracture is, you may have to keep the cast on from three to ten weeks. Little kids' bones heal faster than teens' and adults' because their bodies produce more of the bone-building cells called *osteoblasts*.

What Your Body Does

Your doctor can make sure your bones are in the perfect position to heal correctly, but only your body can actually heal the fracture. Cells in your bones get to work right away, first making a sort of patch where the bone has broken. Cells eat away the dead bone and surround both ends of the broken parts until they're mended. Meanwhile, new blood vessels grow between the two pieces of bone. After three to ten weeks, that bone is healed and is just as strong as before.

What You Can Do to Prevent Broken Bones

Exercising, getting plenty of rest, and eating well are all ways to make sure your bones stay healthy. Another important thing to do is to wear the proper protective gear when playing sports, riding your bike, or skating.

OW, That Really, Really Hurts on the Ouch! Pain Scale

BREAKING YOUR FUNNY BONE

Have you ever banged the outside of your elbow, causing your arm to hurt and feel prickly, tingly, and numb all at the same time? That's called hitting your funny bone; although, it's not a bone and it's not really all that funny! When you hit your funny bone, you're actually knocking the *ulnar nerve*, which controls some of your fingers and some hand movement, into the end of your *humerus bone*, which is the long bone that connects your shoulder to your elbow. Although it can be uncomfortable, that funny feeling goes away after a short while, and nothing is broken.

MAKE YOUR OWN ICE PACK

Grab some ice, put it in a plastic bag, and wrap the bag in a cloth or dishtowel. You can also use a bag of frozen fruit or vegetables. It's never a good idea to apply ice directly to the skin because the ice can stick to your skin.

If you fall while skateboarding, skating, or skiing, you may try to break your fall with your wrists. Wrist guards help prevent wrist injuries by absorbing some of the impact pressure, thus lessening the chance that your wrist bone will break.

This isn't going to end well. It's natural to want to protect yourself from a fall by putting your hands out to brace yourself.

Ack! I Pulled a Muscle!

Muscles move the body. Without them, your bones would remain stationary, your heart wouldn't beat, and your food would never get digested. You have more than 600 of them in your body, and they work by tightening (or contracting) and relaxing (or stretching). Signals from the brain and spinal cord direct these movements so you can do all your everyday functions. A strain or *pulled muscle* happens when you overstretch or partially tear one of these muscles or the tendons that connect them to bones. A muscle can be overstretched or torn if you put the muscle under too much stress, say, while you're lifting something really heavy, or if you exercise without warming up first. Areas of the body that are commonly strained include the back, neck, and legs. After a strain, the injured area will be sore and swollen, perhaps bruised, and it may take up to a week (or longer for a serious strain) for a pulled muscle to heal. You will feel pain, especially when you use the muscle.

First Response

Sometimes, you may not even be aware you strained a muscle until a few hours after hurting it. As soon as you realize you've pulled a muscle, stop using it. Rest, and if you're in a lot of pain, ask for some pain medication from your parents. You can also apply ice packs to help decrease the swelling; however, don't use heat packs until the swelling has gone down completely. More severe strains will require the RICE treatment, which stands for Rest (avoiding any activities that hurt), Ice (placing an ice pack on the area for twenty minutes every

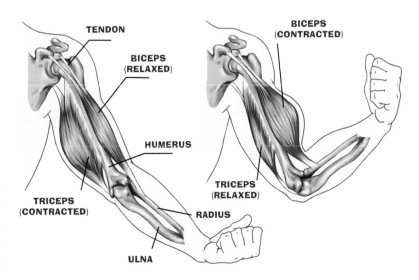

Bones are moved by muscles, which are attached to bones and other muscles by narrow, stretchy cables called tendons.

four hours for two days), Compression (applying a bandage wrap—not too tight!), and Elevation (keeping the hurt area higher than your heart if possible).

What Your Doctor Does

You won't need to go to a doctor unless the pain is unbearable and/or if you're not feeling a little bit better each day.

What Your Body Does

When your muscle is injured, blood vessels widen to allow blood into the injured area, which will cause inflammation. This extra blood sends white blood cells to the scene to remove damaged cells and tissue. Then, new cells begin forming, slowly building over the partial tears in the muscle.

What You Can Do to Prevent Pulled Muscles

The best prevention is to stretch your muscles daily, especially after any exercise. Also, gently warm up before strenuous exercise. For example, run in place for a few minutes before going out to play a sport.

Ow, That Hurts on the Ouch! Pain Scale

WHY DO MY MUSCLES GET SORE?

Your blood brings your muscles extra oxygen when you exercise or otherwise use your muscles. Sometimes, when you're working your muscles harder than usual, they don't get enough oxygen. When that happens, the muscles produce a chemical called *lactic acid*, and it's this acid that makes your muscles sore.

What a Pain! I Have a Sprain!

The bones at your joints (your wrists, knees, elbows, shoulders, ankles) where the body bends and rotates are connected by very strong, elastic bands of tissue called *ligaments*. These hold the bones together so that they stay where they're supposed to while providing a limited range of motion. Although you can sprain any of your joint areas, ankle sprains are most common. If you step down while running and your ankle rolls outward as your foot turns inward, the ligaments on the outside of your ankle bones can overstretch (mild sprain) or partially tear (severe sprain). Unlike a strain, where you may not notice it at first, the pain from a sprain will be immediate. The area will swell, and it will hurt to move your ankle. Your ankle may also bruise. With severe sprains, you will not be able to put weight on the ankle or will feel wobbly walking around on it.

First Response

The first order of business is to stop using the injured body part right away. Then, apply an ice pack for up to twenty minutes at a time every few hours until you can get to a doctor.

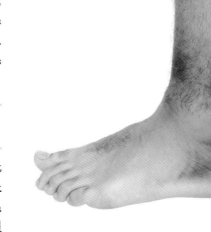

LIGAMENT

What Your Doctor Does

Although mild sprains can be taken care of at home, it's good to get to a doctor or hospital to rule out a broken bone. You often can't tell until you get an X-ray. Once diagnosed, the doctor may give you a temporary cast or splint or boot to wear, and depending on the severity, you may have to use crutches for a week or longer.

What Your Body Does

A sprain will go through the same stages of repair as a strain: inflammation as the blood vessels send blood to the injured area, clean-up as white blood cells break down and dispose of damaged cells, and repair as cells grow and build up the new ligament tissue.

What You Can Do to Prevent Sprains

You can do what are called range-of-motion exercises to strengthen your ankle or other joint that has been sprained. Also, warm up before exercising, and when running, make sure you have the proper shoes for where you'll be exercising.

Ow, That Really Hurts on the Ouch! Pain Scale

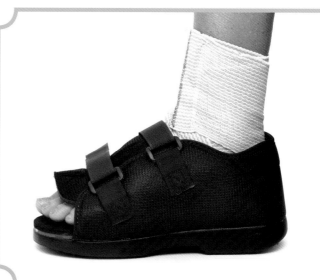

These boots were made for limping around.

Yuck! The Whites of My Eyes Are Pink!

Admit it. You take your eyes for granted. You wake up in the morning, open them, and expect them to work. So, it can cause a bit of worry if you wake up and it feels like someone super-glued your eyes shut. When you finally get the crusty goo out and open your eyes, you look in a mirror and see that they're puffy, red, and oozing a thick, white liquid. Oh yeah, and they're really itchy. You've got pinkeye, and although it's not terribly painful, you won't be going to school today because pinkeye is highly contagious.

Pinkeye usually happens when bacteria or a virus gets into the *conjunctiva*, a clear covering over your eye and the inside of your eyelids that keeps the eye wet with mucus and tears. Through all the itching and oozing, your eyesight should not be affected.

First Response

Place a cool or warm washcloth over your eyes to relieve the itching and get rid of any crust. After that, gently clean your eyelids with warm water, using cotton balls to get rid of the goo. Make sure no one else uses your washcloth and throw away those cotton balls when you're done.

I call pinkeye conjunctivitis!

What Your Doctor Does

First, your doctor will determine whether you have pinkeye or something stuck in your eye. Once the diagnosis is made, he will look closely at your symptoms and figure out if the cause is bacterial or viral. If caused by bacteria, he may prescribe antibiotic eye drops, which will cure you in a few days. If he finds out a virus is causing the infection, there isn't much he can do. Antibiotics don't work against viruses, although there are medications for some of the more serious viral infections of the eye.

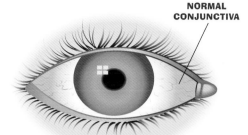

CONJUNCTIVITIS

NORMAL CONJUNCTIVA

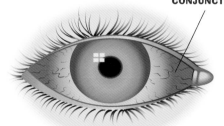

INFLAMED CONJUNCTIVA

What Your Body Does

Even though the conjunctiva is transparent, it contains tiny blood vessels that expand and become more noticeable when your eyes are irritated. That's why your eyes get red when something gets stuck in them or when you rub them too much.

When you get pinkeye, your body goes right to work attacking the bacteria or virus. Within a week, all signs of pinkeye should be gone, even if you don't take any medicine at all. You can go back to school once your symptoms start getting better.

What You Can Do to Prevent Pinkeye

If you know someone at home or at school with pinkeye, avoid shaking that person's hand or sharing a towel with him. If he touches his eyes and then touches your hand, and then you touch your eyes, you'll contaminate yourself! So, even if you're being careful, wash your hands a lot with soap and water, and keep them away from your eyes.

Well, This Is Slightly Annoying on the Ouch! Pain Scale

The same bacteria that cause pinkeye can also give you an ear infection. Meanwhile, viral pinkeye can also cause sore throats.

Ick! I Caught a Cold and Now I'm Sick!

You're sneezing and coughing, your head hurts, your nose is stuffed up, you have no energy, your throat feels itchy, you've got the chills . . . there's a whole lot going wrong with your body when you are infected with one of the more than 200 cold viruses that exist out there. And, as with any virus, medicine won't make it go away. A cold is very infectious, and it's the most common reason kids miss school and adults miss work. In fact, every year in the U.S., there are more than one billion colds caught, and if you don't take good care of yourself, you could catch up to twelve a year!

You get a cold by picking it up from something that has the virus on it (a doorknob, a sink faucet) or from someone who has it already. When a friend with a cold sneezes, coughs, or blows her nose, she shoots virus-infected mucus into the air. If you breathe in one or more of those tiny droplets, the cold virus will stick to the mucus located high up in your nose and start taking over your healthy cells. And if your immune system doesn't fight it off in time, before you know it, you're feeling miserable.

But what you may not realize is that it's not the virus that's making you feel this bad. It's your immune system doing its job that's causing most of the symptoms! Don't worry too much, though. Even though some of the symptoms may last for a week or more, you should be feeling much better in a few days.

First Response

The best things you can do for yourself are get some rest and drink plenty of liquids. Stay in bed, read a book, nap, and otherwise take it easy for a day or two. There is no cure for the cold; however, some medications and treatments may help with the symptoms. Over-the-counter cold and cough medicines take the sting out of the coughing, sneezing, and stuffiness, and the heat, liquid, and salt in chicken soup (or other soup) actually assist in fighting infection. Using a cool mist humidifier at night will help keep your nose and chest clear, making it easier to breathe.

What Your Doctor Does

You won't need to see a doctor for a cold unless you are having difficulty breathing or you don't recover after seven to ten days.

What Your Body Does

I call sneezing sneezing, *although its official name is* sternutation.

Once virus particles get into your nose, the mucus lining of your nasal cavity captures many of them before they can get into your lungs. You'll either swallow that mucus, and your stomach acids will kill the virus particles, or you'll sneeze the virus particles out of your system. The virus pathogens that escape and are able to penetrate the mucus and enter your nasal cavity are attacked by white blood cells called *macrophages*. The virus that escapes the white blood cells enter nasal cells, which is what makes your nose run. The cells that are infected with the virus are then attacked by different white blood cells called *B cells*, and together with helper *T cells*, they produce new cells that act as antibodies against this particular virus. Some of these B cells then remember this virus and will produce antibodies quickly the next time the virus tries to attack.

What You Can Do to Prevent a Cold

The best way to prevent colds is to make sure your immune system is in good shape to fight off the cold viruses that come its way. That means eating well, exercising, and getting enough sleep. A diet rich in fruits and vegetables is proven to ward off infections and sicknesses. It's also important to remember to wash your hands often so virus pathogens don't have a chance to get in your eyes or up your nose. And because we can't always wash our hands, we should keep them away from our face—that includes picking your nose!

This Is Bothering and Irritating Me on the Ouch! Pain Scale

ALL ABOUT SNEEZING

Pollen, dust, bacteria, and viruses can't just sneak up your nose and cause trouble. First, they have to get past your nose hairs, which capture many of these particles before they get too far up your nose. After the nose hairs, there's a layer of thick, sticky mucus that coats the inside of your naval cavities. Many of the particles that make it past your nose hairs get stuck in the mucus and are forced out by your body through sneezes. A sneeze is an involuntary reflex, which means you can't control it or make it happen. When the particles in your nose try to get past its defenses, they trigger the release of histamines (see page 18). This irritates the nerve cells in the nose, which causes the cells to send a message to the brain telling the brain that a foreign substance is somewhere it shouldn't be. Your brain then sends a message to all the muscles needed to produce a sneeze and . . . achoo! A normal sneeze can send dust particles up to twenty feet away, reaching speeds of 35 miles per hour. That's good for you, but not for anyone standing in front of you. So, don't forget to cover your sneezing mouth and nose with your forearm or the inside of your elbow. Don't use your hands or you'll be more likely to spread the germs around!

Catching a sneeze in your hands is not a good idea! Everything you touch could get infected. Instead, sneeze into a tissue or the inside of your forearm.

A sneeze can send germs traveling up to twenty feet away.

Phooey! I've Got the Flu!

If you think you have a cold but you feel a whole lot worse, chances are you have the flu. Every fall and winter, doctors and scientists prepare for flu season, when thousands of people come down with it. Even though the flu causes many of the same symptoms as a cold and is also a virus, it lasts longer and is more severe. For example, your fever will probably be higher than if you just had a cold and your headache will hurt more. Also, the virus affects the respiratory system and can lead to other diseases such as pneumonia. Also, the flu can cause diarrhea and vomiting, especially for kids. With a cold, you're up and about within a few days. The flu will keep you miserable for a week or longer.

First Response

Do the same thing you would as if you had a cold—see page 53.

What Your Doctor Does

Depending on your symptoms, your doctor may tell you to come in for an examination, or, to keep from infecting others, he may ask you to stay home. Severe cases of the flu may require hospitalization in order to replace lost liquids. He may give you medicine that can reduce the time you are ill.

What Your Body Does

Your body will fight the influenza virus the same way it fights a cold virus, but since the virus grows more rapidly, your immune system goes into overdrive trying to kill the pathogens. This means your symptoms are worse and they last longer.

Flu season!

What You Can Do to Prevent the Flu

Unlike a cold, which can be caused by one of hundreds of viruses at any given time, researchers can usually figure out ahead of time which flu viruses are going to cause trouble during flu season (October/November through April/May). Each year, researchers come up with a vaccine (see below) containing small amounts of the three different viruses most likely to make people sick that year. That means, every year before you get sick, doctors recommend getting a flu shot. (Some doctors will give you a nasal spray mist instead.) Also, make sure to regularly wash your hands.

I call the flu influenza.

Ow, That Hurts on the Ouch! Pain Scale

HOW VACCINES WORK

A vaccine delivers a small amount of virus pathogens into your body. (The pathogens you're given are dead, although the nasal spray uses weakened live flu viruses.) Vaccines have eradicated a few deadly diseases such as smallpox and polio. The purpose of a vaccine is to trick your immune system. Upon contact with the dead or weakened viruses, your immune system springs into action. As white blood cells devour the dead or weakened virus particles, lymphocytes are coming in to help remember the virus in case it comes along again. Then, the next time the virus tries to attack, say, when you're actually exposed to strong, live versions of the virus, your immune system will work even more quickly—before the virus has time to spread.

Vaccines can help prevent the flu, but they don't always work perfectly or at all. You could still get a mild form of the flu even if you've had the vaccine. Or you could catch a form of the virus not included in the vaccine.

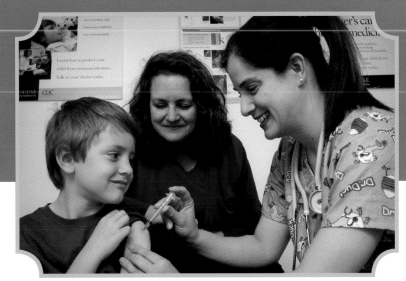

Eek! My Body's a Furnace!

First, you get the chills. Then, you sweat like crazy. You feel weak and all your energy is gone. Your mom or dad takes your temperature, and sure enough, you've got a fever. And a fever is often a sign that germs have attacked. Your body works best at 98.6° Fahrenheit, so your brain controls the thermostat, keeping the temperature just right. Unfortunately, viruses and bacteria also like that temperature, so when they invade, one way your body responds is to turn up the heat, making their new home a lot less friendly for them.

First Response

The best thing you can do if you have a fever is to take it easy for a day or two. In most cases, fevers go away on their own. Plus, since the fever is actually a symptom of your body fighting off germs, you just have to let it do its job. Your body will use more water when you have a fever, so drink plenty of fluids: water, ice pops, and soups are best. If you're really uncomfortable, a parent can give you over-the-counter medication that lowers the fever by blocking the chemicals that tell the brain to turn up the temperature.

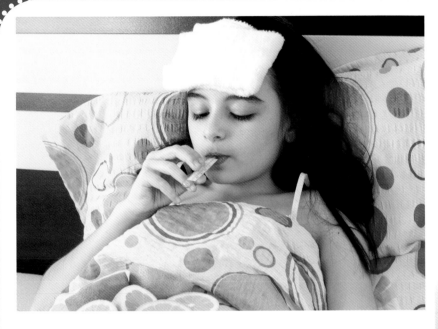

What Your Doctor Does

Fevers are common and go away on their own, so there's no need for a doctor unless you have a really high fever or if you also have a skin rash, diarrhea, and/or are vomiting. These all indicate that something else is going on that the doctor might have to take action on.

What Your Body Does

As your body heats up, you may get the chills and start shivering, even if it's the middle of the summer. This helps the body create more heat. Once your body temperature stops rising, you won't feel cold anymore. When your temperature starts to subside—either on its own or with the help of medication—your body cools down and you begin to feel warm as your body gets rid of the extra heat. You may start sweating and throwing off the covers and you might change into lighter clothing.

What You Can Do to Prevent a Fever

Other than trying to keep your immune system strong so you don't get sick in the first place, there's not much you can do!

This Is Bothering and Irritating Me on the Ouch! Pain Scale

What a Chore! My Throat Is Sore!

Lots of different things can cause a sore throat, such as yelling or singing loudly for a long period of time, air pollution, stomach acid backing up into the throat, and bacteria. However, the most common cause is a cold or the flu. A sore throat includes an itchy feeling in the throat, pain when swallowing, and inflammation and redness.

First Response

- Gargle with salt water. This helps reduce swelling.
- Drink hot fluids such as soup or tea.
- Use a humidifier in your bedroom.
- Using cough drops, a decongestant, or pain medication may help ease the pain.

What Your Doctor Does

No need for a doctor unless you have difficulty breathing, you can't drink, the pain is extremely severe, or you think you may have strep throat (see page 61).

What Your Body Does

See the section on colds on page 53.

What You Can Do to Prevent Sore Throats

See the section on colds on page 53.

This Is Bothering and Irritating Me on the Ouch! Pain Scale

STREP THROAT

One common bacterial throat infection called *strep throat* is caused by a type of bacteria called *Group A streptococci*. The symptoms of strep throat are similar to those of a viral infection, although you may see white or yellow spots on your tonsils and red spots on the roof of your mouth. The good news is that since strep throat is bacterial, your doctor will prescribe an antibiotic that will kill most of the bacteria rather quickly and you'll be back to normal in a few days.

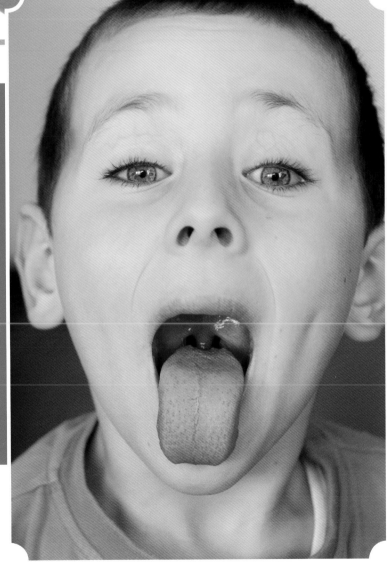

Ouch! There's Something Wrong with My Ear!

Your ear is a complicated organ containing lots of different pieces that work together to detect sound as well as play a key role in keeping your balance. Extremely loud noises can cause ear pain, but usually an earache is caused by an infection. Your infected ear will hurt, especially when you're chewing or lying down, and may appear red or swollen; you may have a fever and you may have trouble hearing. Earaches are the second-most common disease for kids after colds, and 75 percent of children get at least one earache before they're three years old.

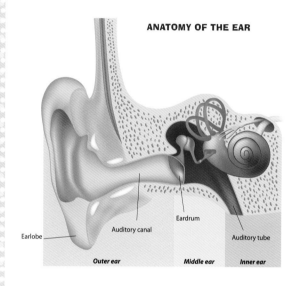

ANATOMY OF THE EAR

Earlobe

Auditory canal

Eardrum

Auditory tube

Outer ear   *Middle ear*   *Inner ear*

First Response

It's not a good idea to place anything (such as a finger) in your ear to help relieve the pain. Nothing you stick in there will help at all. Depending on how serious the infection is, a few days of rest may be all you need. A visit to the doctor is recommended.

What Your Doctor Does

Your doctor will look inside your ear with an instrument called an *otoscope*, which is a combination flashlight/magnifier that lets your doctor see what's going on in there. He may prescribe a mild pain reliever and an antibiotic.

What Your Body Does

The ear has three main sections: the *outer* or *external*, which funnels sound toward its sensors inside; the *middle*, which contains the *eardrum* that picks up the sound waves and vibrates; and the *inner*, which transforms the vibrations into nerve impulses that travel to the brain. Most earaches are due to inflammation, infection, and/or fluid buildup in the middle ear in a pocket of air behind the eardrum. When you have a cold, an allergic reaction, or a throat infection, a tube that

connects the throat to the middle ear, which is responsible for moving air in and out, can get blocked. A blocked tube provides a perfect setting for germs to hang out and grow. The immune system comes to the rescue by filling up the area with fluid, which fights the germs. This fluid makes your ear feel like it's going to explode like a balloon.

What You Can Do to Prevent Earaches

Like colds, earaches are difficult to prevent since germs are everywhere. If you stay away from people with colds and wash your hands regularly, you'll have a better chance of avoiding this annoying condition.

Ow, That Hurts on the Ouch! Pain Scale

An infection of the outer ear is called *swimmer's ear.* When water or other debris (sand, dirt, etc.) gets stuck in the ear canal, bacteria have more of a chance to grow—leading to redness, swelling, and pain. Scratching the area can also lead to infection. Antibiotic ear drops usually clear up the mess within a week. If you go swimming and get water stuck in your ear, try to get it out by hopping on one foot while tipping your head to the side and gently tugging on your earlobe.

WHAT MAKES ME DIZZY?

Each of your ears has three liquid-filled tubes in it. The liquid swishes when you spin and nerves in your ear send a message to the brain that you are spinning. Stop suddenly and the liquid keeps swishing for a moment longer, giving your brain the wrong message that you are still moving. You can also get dizzy when you stand up too quickly from lying down. When lying down, your blood is spread out evenly throughout your body. If you quickly pop out of bed, the sudden movement, along with gravity, pulls blood down and away from your brain. The brain can't work without blood, so for a moment or two, your body functions stop working properly and you feel dizzy.

Pull Over! I'm Going to Puke!

You're sitting in the backseat of the car on the way to Grandma's house. You're reading a book when all of a sudden you feel dizzy. Your stomach feels like it's on a roller coaster, and you're certain you're going to be sick. You don't have the flu or other disease, but you just caught a case of motion sickness. Scientists aren't completely certain why this happens to some people; however, one theory is that it happens when your eyes, ears, and other parts of your body send confusing messages to your brain. So, for instance, your eyes that are reading the book in the car tell your brain that you're not moving because the words on the page are staying relatively stable. However, your inner ear, sensing the car accelerating or making turns on a winding road, tells your brain you are moving. These conflicting messages convince the brain that there must be some sort of poison attacking the body, since either your eyes or your ears are hallucinating (experiencing things that aren't there), and hallucinating is often a symptom of poisoning. So the brain sends messages telling your body to get rid of the "poison" by puking, or making you want to. Motion sickness can happen in a car, train, plane, boat (where it's called being sea sick), or even on an amusement park ride. This can happen whenever you feel that you're moving but you can't see it, you can see that you're moving but can't feel it, or if you feel and see that you're moving but the same message isn't getting to the brain.

First Response

- If you're in a car, ask to pull over. Walk around a bit and grab a plastic bag for when you continue your journey just in case you need to be sick into it.
- Try chewing gum.
- If you're facing backward on a boat or train, see if you can switch seats so that you're facing forward.
- Look out the window.
- If on a boat, train, or plane, move your seat so you're in the center, away from windows and where the movement back and forth is less.
- Ask your parents to get some over-the-counter medications you can take that will relieve the symptoms.

What Your Doctor Does

You won't need to see a doctor for motion sickness; however, if you get motion sickness fairly easily, your doctor may ask to see you to make sure your inner ears are okay.

What Your Body Does

Once you've convinced your eyes that you are indeed moving, your brain will send out messages that the "poison" invading your system is gone, and your symptoms should go away.

What You Can Do to Prevent Motion Sickness

If you think you're going to get sick the next time you're traveling, prepare ahead of time. Ask your parents to bring anti–motion sickness medication. Find a seat either next to a window or in the center of the vehicle (on a boat, train, or plane), and whenever you begin to feel dizzy, do what you can to make sure your brain is not getting confusing messages by looking up from your book and looking out a window.

This Is Bothering and Irritating Me on the Ouch! Pain Scale

Oh Gee! I Have an Allergy!

To be *allergic* to something means that although most people have no trouble with a certain food or other item, you do. You can be *allergic* to food, medicine, pollen, dust particles, and more, and your body's reaction to these things can be mild or severe. A mild reaction includes a runny nose, sneezing, and itchy eyes, throat, and ears. A severe reaction includes difficulty breathing and low blood pressure, which means your blood isn't flowing through your arteries and veins at the proper speed.

First Response

For mild allergic reactions, you need to get away from whatever is causing the allergy. For severe allergies, you have to get to a hospital right away, or if your parents or teachers know about your allergy, they will have medicine for you with them, which they will give you.

What Your Doctor Does

If it seems like you have allergies but can't figure out what you're allergic to, you'll be taken to an allergy specialist who will do a series of tests to

identify the allergen. The doctor will ask if anyone else in your family has any allergies since they can be hereditary. He will also take a blood sample to be tested or perform a skin test where a small amount of different allergy-causing particles in liquid form are placed on the skin. (He will scratch the skin before dripping the liquid on it.) If your allergies are mild, you may be able to live without any medication at all; although you may find some relief in an over-the-counter antihistamine. People with severe allergies may need allergy shots. They will also have to be very careful not to encounter the allergy-causing item and carry around medicine to give themselves if they do meet up with it.

What Your Body Does

Unlike most of the things in this book that hurt, allergies happen when your immune system makes a mistake. Your blood carries special white blood cells called lymphocytes that create antibodies that kill bacteria and viruses. But when you have an allergy, your immune system treats something harmless as if it's the enemy. So, for example, if you're allergic to peanuts and accidentally eat one, lymphocytes create too many antibodies, which causes an immune cell called a *mast cell* to release a chemical into the bloodstream called *histamine*. If your allergy is mild, histamine will cause your eyes to get itchy, your nose to run, your throat to get sore, and/or your skin to break out in a rash, among other things. If you have a severe reaction, your immune system will overreact everywhere in your body. Your blood pressure could drop and your breathing tubes could swell, making breathing difficult, and more. This is called *anaphylaxis*, and it can be fatal if not treated immediately.

What You Can Do to Prevent Allergies

The only thing you can really do is avoid whatever it is you're allergic to.

From *Well, This Is Slightly Annoying* to *OW, That Really, Really Hurts* on the Ouch! Pain Scale

COMMON ITEMS PEOPLE ARE ALLERGIC TO

Animal dander (dead skin cells)
Animal fur
Beans
Berries
Celery
Corn
Dust mite poop
Eggs
Grass and weeds
Insect poisons (bee stings)
Milk
Mold
Peanuts
Penicillin
Seafood
Soy
Tree and flower pollen
Wool

Blech! I Have a Stomachache!

There's a lot going on in your stomach, which is why there are many different reasons why it might be hurting you. Your stomach, also known as the abdomen, belly, or tummy, is the area between your chest and hip bones. It's home to several organs including the intestines, kidneys, liver, and more—all held together by a bag-like membrane called the *peritoneum*. Your stomach is in charge of absorbing and digesting food. If it feels sore, crampy, or if you have sharp pains, one of the following may be the reason.

Constipation

Your stomach may hurt and become swollen if you haven't pooped for a while. Constipation can happen if you don't drink enough water during the day or if you're not getting enough fiber. Stress or too much dairy in your diet can also be factors. Before going to a doctor, try increasing your intake of water and fiber-rich foods such as fruits and vegetables. Exercise also helps prevent constipation.

Stomach Flu

If you have stomach cramps, diarrhea, and a fever, and you feel like you're going to puke, you may have *gastroenteritis*, which is a fancy word for stomach flu. This isn't the same as the traditional flu, but it is usually caused by a virus, and it will make you feel pretty sick for a day or two. Since it's a virus, not only is it contagious, but there's also no cure, so you're going to have to wait for your body to kill off the virus before feeling better. (Gastroenteritis can also be caused by bacteria, in which case, antibiotics can be used to help make you feel better.)

Indigestion

Symptoms of indigestion include a stomachache and a burning feeling from your chest up to the back of your throat. The burning occurs when stomach acid splashes up into your esophagus, which also might leave a yucky taste in your mouth. This can happen when you eat too much or too quickly or if you eat something that's too spicy or otherwise doesn't agree with you. You might also have to burp a lot and may feel like puking. You won't have to see a doctor for this unless you're getting indigestion a lot for no particular reason. You can avoid indigestion by eating slowly and avoiding foods that bother you. Fried foods and foods with lots of fat are often culprits.

Food Poisoning

This sometimes happens when you eat food with harmful bacteria in it. This could be food that has spoiled or been left out of the refrigerator too long or meat that hasn't been properly cooked. As your stomach reacts to this bacteria, you will feel waves of pain and you'll probably puke or have a bad case of diarrhea. These are signals from the body that your abdomen has a fight on its hands. Sometimes food poisoning is confused with the stomach flu, especially since you may not get sick until hours after you ate the contaminated food.

Stomachache cures from the past include drinking urine in medieval Europe, eating dirt in precolonial America, and drinking a glass of water full of millipedes in seventeenth-century England.

Appendicitis

This is a disease of your appendix, a small organ connected to your large intestine that doesn't serve much of a purpose. Symptoms include a pain or cramp right around your belly button that hurts more when you move or cough. You may also have a slight fever and have to puke. You may confuse appendicitis with the stomach flu or food poisoning; however, if the pain persists, a trip to the doctor is a good idea. She will examine you, and if the appendix is infected, you will have to have an operation to remove it. Don't worry, though. Your body can work perfectly well without it.

Stress

If you're worried about something—a big math test, an argument you had with your mom, getting in trouble for something you did at school—you may feel sick to your stomach or have a bad headache. This is called *stress*, and it can affect your body in negative ways. Your best medicine for stress is to talk to an adult about what's going on, take care of your body by getting plenty of rest, exercise, and good food, and relax by breathing in and out slowly and deeply on a regular basis, especially when the stress feels overwhelming.

PUKING

Throwing up is an involuntary reaction like sneezing—you can't help or control it. If you eat spoiled or improperly cooked food, overeat, or are sick, your brain sends a message to your stomach and diaphragm muscles to contract and come together quickly in order to push the contents of your stomach up through your esophagus and out your mouth.

From *Ow, That Hurts* to *OW, That Really Really Hurts* on the Ouch! Pain Scale

Oh No! My Head's Going to Explode!

A headache can be on one side of your head or both. In the back of your head or up front. It can travel down your neck or send sharp knife-like pain into your forehead. The pain can be there constantly or throb like waves coming and going. A headache can be a minor bother or can sap you of all your energy. Headaches come for all kinds of reasons, and while some are not very serious, others can signal a life-threatening illness.

First off, it's not even your brain that's feeling the pain—the brain and skull have no pain nerve cells—but rather it's the area just outside your skull, which is jam-packed with nerve cells, blood vessels, and muscles. Under certain circumstances, the muscles and blood vessels swell, putting pressure on the nerves, which sends the pain messages to the brain. Lots of different things can cause a headache, including staying up too late, spending too much time in front of a TV or computer screen, stress and worry, strong smells such as perfumes and smoke, caffeine, allergies, certain foods, dehydration, infection, or trauma to the head.

First Response

- Take pain medication.
- Stop what you're doing or get away from strong odors.

- Place a cool cloth across your forehead.
- Take a nap, UNLESS you have had a recent trauma to the head. (If you've banged your head, you may have a concussion and taking a nap if you have a concussion could be dangerous! Read more about concussions on page 74.)

What Your Doctor Does

There's no need for a doctor unless your headache is extremely painful and doesn't go away, if your vision is affected (this could happen if you bumped your head), or if your thinking is clouded. Your doctor will run some tests to try and determine what's causing the pain and what will help you feel better.

What Your Body Does

After some time, the swelling of the blood vessels will go down, releasing the pressure on the nerves, and your head will stop hurting.

What You Can Do to Prevent Headaches

You can limit the severity of most common headaches by changing your diet, getting more sleep, napping when you feel a headache coming on, doing some simple relaxation exercises, or taking pain medication. If you feel a headache coming on, take a break from what you're doing, eating, or drinking.

Past cultures had many "cures" for headaches, including drilling the skull to release the evil spirits that were supposedly making your head hurt. Surprisingly, some actually survived this operation.

From *Barely Even Notice It* to *Ow, That Really Hurts* on the Ouch! Pain Scale

TWO OF THE MOST COMMON TYPES OF HEADACHES

Tension: Most headaches fall under this category. You'll feel a constant pain or dull ache around the head, especially at the temples or the back of the head. Tension headaches happen when you squeeze your head and neck muscles too hard for too long, which is something people tend to do when they're stressed out, depressed, not well rested, sick with a cold or flu, hungry, and/or thirsty. Tension headaches can last for as little as thirty minutes or as long as a day or two.

Migraine: These headaches are more painful than tension headaches. The pain tends to come in waves, throbbing on one or both sides of your head. You might get dizzy and throw up, and you will be sensitive to light, noise, and even smells. Migraines are caused by blood vessels in your head expanding and getting inflamed. Not everyone gets migraines, but since they can be inherited, those who have a parent who gets migraines may be more prone to them.

BRAIN FREEZE

You get brain freeze when you eat something really cold such as ice cream or an ice pop. When the cold food touches the roof of your mouth, nerves that control how much blood flows to your head cause blood vessels to swell. This puts pressure on the nerves just outside your skull—causing the pain. The pain goes away within a minute or two, although some say putting your thumb on the roof of your mouth or drinking warm water will make brain freeze go away more quickly.

CONCUSSION

When you get bonked, bumped, or banged on the head and get a concussion, your brain, which is cushioned by spinal fluid, has actually moved inside your skull, perhaps even hitting into the inside of your skull. This changes the way your brain functions for a short time, and you may feel dizzy, nauseated, confused, have blurred vision, or you may even be unable to remember what happened right before or after the injury. You could be knocked unconscious for a time. After a thorough examination where your doctor will test your memory and concentration skills and perhaps order a CAT scan (a 3-D brain X-ray) or MRI (magnetic resonance imaging), you will either be hospitalized so medical professionals can observe you or be sent home with instructions on how to take care of yourself. If you think you have a concussion, it's important to seek medical attention right away.

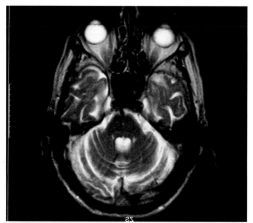

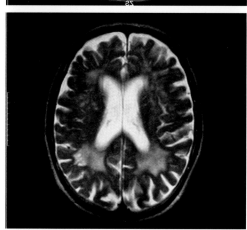

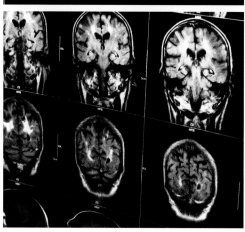

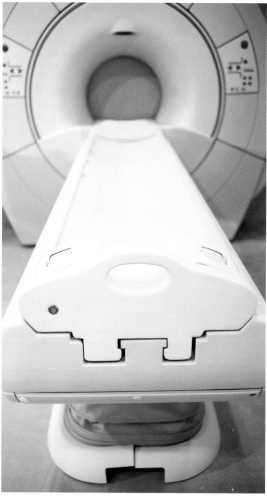

A CAT scan is an X-ray that turns around you and takes pictures of "slices" of you. They are best used for taking images of bones, lungs, the chest, and for cancer detection. An MRI uses magnets and radio waves to create images of tissue, ligaments, tendons, the spinal cord, the brain, and other "soft" tissue in your body.

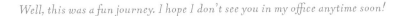

Well, this was a fun journey. I hope I don't see you in my office anytime soon!

Acknowledgments

The author would like to thank the following for their expertise in helping to create a healthy book: Richard Hudspeth MD, Melissa Gerber, Anthony Owsley, Lynn Weingarten, Charles Nurnberg, and Jeremy Nurnberg. Any mistakes in the text are my own.

Photo Credits

Unless listed below, the images in this book were created by Anthony Owsley.

Bruce Wetzel and Harry Schaefer/National Cancer Institute: page 18
Center for Disease Control: page 55, bottom; page 57
Ecorahul: page 20
National Cancer Institute: page 21
Public Domain Image from Encyclopédie ou Dictionnaire Raisonné des Sciences, des Arts et des Métiers: page 72
Shutterstock: page 10, bottom right; page 13, top left; page 15; page 16, top, middle, bottom right; page 17, bottom; page 18, bottom; page 20, top right, middle; page 21, top left, right, bottom; page 22; page 24, bottom; page 25, top; page 29; page 30, bottom; page 31; page 32; page 33, bottom; page 35; page 36, right; page 37, top right; page 39; page 41; page 42; page 43, bottom center; page 45, top left, top right; page 47, bottom; page 48; page 49, top right; page 50, bottom right; page 51, bottom; page 52, top right; page 56, bottom; page 59; page 61; page 62; page 64, top right; page 65, top left; page 67; page 69; page 74
USDA: page 40, bottom

Glossary

abrasion. The rubbing, wearing, or grinding of the surface layer of skin cells.

allergen. Normally harmless substance that causes an allergic reaction in someone.

allergy. Overreaction (hypersensitivity) of the body's immune system to exposure to substances or situations that don't affect the average person.

anaphylaxis. Severe bodily reaction to contact with an allergen.

antibiotic. Medicine created to destroy pathogens in the body.

antibody. T-shaped cell created by B cells to fight a specific bacterial infection or virus by binding to it.

antigen. Any foreign substance in the body that causes an immune response.

antihistamine. Medicine created to counteract the release of histamine in the body in order to prevent allergy attacks.

appendicitis. Inflammation of the appendix.

appendix. Hollow tube attached to the large intestine that has no digestive function.

artery. Blood vessel that carries blood away from the heart and through the body.

B cell. Type of white blood cell (lymphocyte) that produces antibodies that attach to specific antigens.

bacteria. Single-celled organisms that can live on their own. Some cause disease.

blood. The fluid that circulates in the heart, arteries, capillaries, and veins, bringing nourishment and oxygen and taking away waste products from all parts of the body.

bone. Any of the hard parts of the skeleton of a vertebrate.

bone marrow. Soft tissue that fills the spaces of most bones. Where blood cells are formed.

brain. Organ that's the central control point for the nervous system. The origin of thought.

bruise. Injury in which the skin is not broken but the blood vessels underneath are, causing discoloration of the skin.

capillary. Tiny blood vessel that connects arteries and veins.

CAT scan. Three-dimensional X-ray image of tissue in the body.

cell. Basic building blocks of living things.

cilia. Tiny hairlike structures on the surface of some cells.

circulatory system. Consists of the heart, a network of blood vessels, and blood. Supplies essentials to cells, removes waste, and helps fight infection.

coagulate. To clot or become thickened into a mass.

concussion. Injury to the brain resulting from a hard blow.

conjunctiva. Clear covering that lines the inner surface of the eyelids and keeps the eye moist.

conjunctivitis. See *pinkeye*.

constipation. Delayed or infrequent passage of hardened stools.

contusion. Injury to body tissue that doesn't result in bleeding. Bruise.

cytoplasm. Jellylike material that fills a cell.

dermatitis. Inflammation of the skin that causes itching, redness, swelling, and blistering.

dermatologist. Doctor who specializes in diseases of the skin.

dermis. Layer of skin below the epidermis composed of connective tissue.

diarrhea. Abnormally frequent evacuations of loose and fluid stools.

digestive system. Consists of the mouth, esophagus, stomach, intestines, liver, and other organs. Responsible for taking in and processing food so it can be used by the body.

disease. Disorder caused by one or more body system malfunctioning.

eczema. Skin rash that causes redness, itching, and sometimes, oozing lesions.

endocrine system. Consists of a number of glands that release chemicals called hormones, which act as messengers. Responsible for controlling many processes including reproduction and growth.

epidermis. Outer layer of skin, consisting of flattened dead cells.

fever. Abnormally high body temperature, usually caused by infection.

flu. Short for *influenza*. Any of the several contagious viral diseases that cause fever, aches and pains, and respiratory or intestinal symptoms.

fracture. Broken bone.

fungus. Spore-producing organism such as mold, mildew, mushrooms, and yeasts.

gastroenteritis. Inflammation of the lining of the stomach that causes nausea, vomiting, diarrhea, and cramps.

germ. General term for a microorganism that causes disease.

gland. Tissue or organ that produces a substance, such as sweat, which is released into or onto the body.

granulocyte. White blood cell formed in bone marrow.

headache. Pain in the head.

hemoglobin. Protein in red blood cells that transports oxygen throughout the body.

histamine. Substance released by cells that triggers inflammation.

hives. Allergic condition in which the skin breaks out in red patches that itch.

immune system. Body system that protects the body from disease-causing organisms.

immunity. When the body is able to resist an infectious disease usually through natural resistance, vaccination, or a previous attack of the disease.

indigestion. Difficulty digesting food that leads to an uncomfortable feeling in the upper stomach.

infection. When germs invade the body and multiply.

inflammation. Redness, swelling, heat, and pain produced by the body as a defensive reaction to injury or infection.

influenza. See *flu*.

integumentary system. Consists of the skin, hair, and nails. Responsible for protecting the body.

larynx. The voice box. Located between the throat and trachea.

ligament. Bands of connective tissue that attach bones to one another.

lymphatic system. Consists of lymph nodes, tonsils, thymus, and spleen. Responsible for returning fluids and proteins to the blood and destroying pathogens.

lymphocyte. White blood cell formed in lymph nodes and becomes either a T cell or B cell.

macrophage. White blood cell that targets and eats pathogens.

magnetic resonance imaging (MRI). Computerized image of internal body tissues created using magnetic fields and radio waves.

mast cell. Type of cell that stores and releases histamine and plays a role in allergies.

membrane. Thin skin-like covering.

microorganism. Organism that can only be seen with a microscope.

migraine. Severe headache that can cause vomiting, dizziness, and abnormal sensitivity to light, noise, and even smells.

monocyte. White blood cell produced in the spleen that turns into a macrophage.

motion sickness. Sickness caused by travel in car, airplane, or ship that is characterized by nausea and vomiting.

mucous membrane. Skin-like covering that lines some tissue and organs such as the digestive tract.

mucus. Thick substance secreted by the lining of the respiratory and digestive systems that moistens, protects, and cleans.

muscle. Organ that uses energy to contract in order to move the body.

muscle strain. When a muscle or its attaching tendons is overstretched or partially torn.

muscular system. Consists of more than 640 skeletal muscles that are attached to bones by tendons. Responsible for moving the body.

nasal cavity. Hollow space behind the nose through which air flows during breathing.

nervous system. Consists of the brain, spinal cord, nerves, and sense receptors. Processes information and sends instructions throughout the body.

neuron. Elongated cell that transmits nerve signals throughout the body.

neutrophil. White blood cell that targets and consumes pathogens.

nucleus. Control center of a cell that contains the cell's genetic material.

organ. Body part that is made up of two or more tissues and has a specific role.

osteoblast. Bone-forming cell.

otoscope. Instrument used to magnify and light up the interior of the ear.

parasite. Organism that lives on or in another organism and benefits from it.

pathogen. Microorganism such as bacterium or virus that causes disease.

phagocyte. Large white blood cell that engulfs debris and germs.

phagocytosis. Destruction of germs by phagocytes.

pinkeye. Highly contagious infection of the conjunctiva.

plasma. Clear liquid part of blood.

platelet. Cell fragment carried by the blood that plays a key role in blood clotting.

protozoan. Any of the group of tiny animals such as amoebas that is single-celled.

pus. Whitish fluid that contains dead phagocytes.

rabies. Viral infection that affects the nervous system. Usually caused by a bite from an animal already infected.

rash. Breaking out of the skin in spots.

red blood cell. Cell of the blood that contains hemoglobin and carries oxygen from the lungs to the tissue.

reproductive system. Responsible for creating new life.

respiratory system. Consists of lungs and air passages in head and neck. Responsible for breathing—moving air in and out.

saliva. Liquid secreted into the mouth by salivary glands. Begins the breakdown of food.

salivary gland. Responsible for releasing saliva into the mouth.

scab. Hardened covering of blood or pus that forms over a wound.

scar. Mark left on the skin by the healing process of an injury.

serum. Clear, yellowish liquid inside a blister.

skeletal system. Consists of 206 bones, cartilage, and ligaments. Responsible for surrounding and protecting the internal organs, giving shape to the body, and allowing the body to move.

skin. Body's biggest organ that covers bone, organs, and blood.

skin graft. Medical procedure in which a piece of healthy skin is removed and transferred to an area of the body that has been burned.

sneeze. Sudden, noisy, and violent action of forcing the breath out through the nose or mouth.

spinal cord. Nervous tissue that extends from the brain along the back in the cavity of the backbone that carries nerve impulses to and from the brain.

sprain. Overstretching or partial tearing of a ligament.

strep throat. Infection of the throat caused by *Group A streptococci.*

subcutaneous fat. Bottom layer of skin made up mostly of fat. Provides insulation against cold or heat as well as cushioning.

suture. Strand or fiber used to sew up a cut that's too large for a bandage.

swelling. Abnormal enlargement caused by inflammation.

swimmer's ear. Inflammation of the outer ear.

system. Group of organs working together to perform a specific task.

T cell. White blood cell that fights infection.

Tendon. Band of connective tissue that attaches muscles to bones and to one another.

tension headache. Mild to moderate head pain.

tissue. Group of cells that are similar and perform a specific task.

urinary system. Consists of two kidneys, the bladder, and the ureter. Responsible for making and transporting waste urine out of the body.

urushiol. Oily, toxic liquid from poison ivy, oak, and sumac.

vaccine. Injection of killed or weakened microbes meant to create immunity to a disease.

vein. Blood vessel that carries blood from the tissue back to the heart.

virus. Tiny nonliving agent that can cause disease by multiplying within living cells.

white blood cell. Type of cell found in the blood that is involved in defending the body against pathogens.

Index